ROHNA MEMORIES II

HMT Rohna

ROHNA MEMORIES II

EYEWITNESS TO TRAGEDY

Michael Walsh

iUniverse, Inc.
New York Bloomington Shanghai

Rohna Memories II
Eyewitness to Tragedy

Copyright © 2008 by Michael T. Walsh

iUniverse books may be ordered through booksellers or by contacting:

iUniverse
1663 Liberty Drive
Bloomington, IN 47403
www.iuniverse.com
1-800-Authors (1-800-288-4677)

ISBN: 978-0-595-49679-2 (pbk)
ISBN: 978-0-595-61206-2 (ebk)

Printed in the United States of America

I would like to dedicate this book to my mother, Harriet, and father, Raymond. Both lead me to this point in life. It was through them that I learned to appreciate family.

My father spent his entire career in the Air Force, retiring in 1964 as a Lieutenant Colonel. During WWII, while serving as the navigator of a B-17, his bomber was shot down over occupied France. He and two others from the crew evaded the Germans, finally returning to England with the help of the French Underground. It was through him that I learned self discipline and gained an appreciation of the military's role in our American freedom.

My mother was a nurturer with an artistic mind. She always supported her three boys and gave us encouragement in whatever we did. After the early death of my oldest brother, Raymond, Jr., my mother was never the same. Even through that tough time, she was a very positive force in both my brother Leo's life and mine. Our joy was her joy, she loved her family deeply. It is her love of family and artistic talent that that have lead me down my life's path.

Contents

Acknowledgments

Everyone that either sent me their stories or sat down with me for an interview deserves heartfelt thanks. Also a special acknowledgement goes to friends like Chuck Finch, Don Fortune, Carlton Jackson and John Fievet, Sr. who contributed time and materials to this project. My greatest cheerleader and contributor was Ruth Canney. Her knowledge of the people and excellent records added much to the book. Mike Scott and Jim Canney, Ruth's son, were also very helpful with the interviews in this book. I would also like to thank John Fievet, Jr., the current president of the *Rohna* Survivors Memorial Association for making many materials available to me.

Cover Photo
by Robert Uth/Courtesy of the American Battle Monuments Commission.

With thanks to:

Mike Conley
Director of Public Affairs
American Battle Monuments Commission
and
Carole Simpson
Office Manager/Executive Assistant
ABMC Mediterranean Region

Separate and special thanks go to my stepfather, Don Dupre. It was through him that I first learned of the *Rohna*. He has been my companion and friend from the very beginning. Finally, I'd like to thank my wife Danette, daughter Mary, and son Tim who have supported me throughout the years that it has taken to complete this book.

Introduction

During World War II, America lost thousands of soldiers to the sea. Many are familiar with the tragedy of the *U.S.S. Arizona*, bombed while docked at Pearl Harbor on December 7, 1941; also with the sinking of the *U.S.S. Indianapolis*, returning from her secret atomic bomb mission in August of 1945. But it is unlikely that you've heard the story of *HMT Rohna*, a British transport ship used to carry American fighting men to the China-Burma-India theatre in November of 1943. Why? The sinking of the *Rohna* represented an historic first. It was the first U.S. ship destroyed by a guided missile in the history of warfare. Its destruction by those means was deemed classified, so that even families who lost fathers, brothers, and sons were not told the circumstances of their loved ones deaths.

The *Rohna* began its fateful journey on November 25, 1943 at the port of Oran in Algiers, North Africa. There, over 2,000 American enlisted men, American and British officers, Red Cross staff, and Indian Lascar crew gathered to embark on the ship that was to carry them to Bombay, India as part of convoy KMF-26. From the beginning, there was a sense of unease about the ship. And in the end, 1,015 American men lost their lives—another historic milestone representing the greatest loss of American military personnel at sea, ever.

On November 26, 1943 the 24-ship convoy was in the Mediterranean as three Luftwaffe squadrons descended on them. The men on board each ship knew that the possibility of attack was great, but no one guessed that the German bombers carried the latest in technology … rocket-propelled, radio-controlled Henschel HS-293 glide bombs. British, American, and free French fighter planes rushed from bases in North Africa to aid the besieged convoy. Finally a Heinkel 177 bombardier set his sights on the *Rohna*, guiding the payload with deadly accuracy.

Once in the water, many men found their struggle was just beginning. They fought to get clear of the sinking *Rohna*, lest its death throes pull them under too. They battled to secure lifebelts, and to grab at pieces of the destroyed ship for support. They could do nothing about the German fighters targeting them, but they hoped to survive long enough to be saved. The other ships in the convoy were engaged with fighting the enemy and could not immediately split off to save the *Rohna* crew. As a result, many men were in the water for hours before being rescued. Many died waiting.

The search for survivors ended in the early morning hours of November 27. The American minesweeper *U.S.S. Pioneer* on escort duty was responsible for saving the majority of men. The small ship managed to rescue over 600 survivors from the doomed transport. Finally, the rescue ships laden with those plucked from the sea turned towards land, where food, clean clothes, and medical supplies were waiting. For most, the tragedy of November 26, 1943 was not discussed in detail until 50 years later, at the first meeting of *Rohna* survivors in Gatlinburg, Tennessee. It is clear that this single experience changed the lives of all of those who lived through it.

> *"I lost five good friends that night … it changed me very, very much … it was a big big difference from before what happened and right after … why would we live and the others didn't? To see so many men die in just a few hours is not an easy thing to take … I've never explained to anyone just how bad it was … it was a horrible thing to see."*
>
> Bill Caskey

This book is dedicated to those involved in this incident. Many survivors still suffer deep mental and physical wounds. As I have grown to know many of these men it is amazing to see how vividly these memories have been etched into their minds, frozen in time. Most came home from the war to live happy and productive lives but the scars never fully healed ... always there under the surface. This book is a chance to tell their stories in full. Some recollections conflict with that of others ... it doesn't matter. These are their stories, as told by them.

Rohna Memories II is a continuation of my work to document this largely untold historical event.

AN INTERVIEW WITH ACE BALDASSARI

Rohna Survivor

Edited for readability

Baldassari: My real name is Azio. I was born in Hoboken, New Jersey. When I was four, I moved uptown to Jersey City, New Jersey. I lived in Jersey City, New Jersey up to the day I was inducted into the service. The doctor who examined me was my family physician. So I got a real brief and cursory examination. He took my temperature and said, "You're fine." And in I went. I reported to Newark, was inducted, got a good physical. I was then injected, inoculated, and issued clothing. Got aboard a train and we headed from Newark to Indianapolis, Indiana for Camp Atterbury. I was fortunate enough to be a supernumerary. They had picked out 250 men and then I was amongst one of the supernumeraries. In fact, I was the very last. Then they put us aboard a train and we headed for good old Indiana, Camp Atterbury. After 8-10 hours, we got into Indianapolis in the dead of the morning and oh, it was cold. We were greeted, marched into barracks, assigned bunks, and then we proceeded to be trained as soldiers and linemen. After just about a year, we went down to Tennessee for maneuvers and then we were instructed that we were going to go overseas. We went to Norfolk, Virginia, got aboard a liberty ship, 31 days aboard the liberty

5

ship into Oran Harbor. We disembarked and we were stationed in Oran until we set sail for our trip to India.

One thing I remember aboard the liberty ship, no one got anything but a saltwater shower. But being as how I worked aboard it, I went into the laundry and found the washtub that was heated with a steam coil and served with fresh water. So every night about 2:00 or 3:00 in the morning, I was in there enjoying a little freshwater bath.

Oran was bitter cold. I was making myself little gasoline stoves to heat up K-rations. I made one; it worked fine. Then I made another one; so I had one going and one waiting. The one that was running, ran out of fuel and I put it aside and then lit the other one. When I went back to fuel up the first one, I didn't know the fire there wasn't out. I poured a can of gas into it and it exploded. So I was afire. I swept up some sand to put the fire out and in the sand, I picked up gasoline too. So I had fire on my arms, fire on the shirt, fire on my hair. I backed up over my bunk, got my feet under me and then rolled out of the tent and I sustained 2nd and 3rd degree burns on my hand, 1st and 2nd degree burns on my face and neck. So the medic dressed me up with a nice big "boxing glove". The next morning it was throbbing, it was letting me know that I had something going on there. So I said, "You'd better get me to the hospital, because something's going on." I went to the hospital and they found a big blister and they peeled me like a banana. Then they put me in bed and they started treating the burn. After three or four days when it started to heal, they taped it up here (near my face) and I couldn't stand the smell. Now I'm one-armed.

Because I could speak and understand Italian, they assigned me to 25 prisoners of war that worked as orderlies around the surgical ward tent. We cleaned the tent, the top of the tent, the roof of the tent. We swept up and mopped up and they fed me and they shaved me and they bathed me. Until one day they said, "You know, Sergeant, your outfit's leaving." I said, "Whoa, I'd better let my company commander know." So I asked them to notify my company commander to come down and see me. He came down to see me and he says, "What's up, Sarge?" I said, "I understand you're leaving." "How'd you find out?" I said, "The POWs told me." He said, "What?" "Well, what's your problem?" I said, "I want to go with you. I may never see you guys again and I want to go with you. I trained with you and I want to go with you." So he called in the commanding officer of the hospital and he said, "Is this man ready to go?" The colonel came over to me and he said "How's your hand feel, Sergeant?" I said, "Fine. Yeah, see it's fine." He said, "Well, make a fist." I made a fist, because the crust on my knuckles all cracked. But he took a look at it and he said, "Alright, let him go." So I was discharged from the hospital that night about 6:00 in the evening.

I hitchhiked through and I got to the pier on the 25th and they were loading. So I loaded up with them onto the Rajula I was told, "No, you've got to go back. Your outfit's on the Rohna." Fortunately for me, or unfortunately, I went back to the Rohna. There I was with untied shoes, fatigue trousers, shorts, and a fatigue jacket, which I couldn't button and nothing else. So we set sail that morning about 8:00 in the morning. They said go over to the box and pick yourself up a life belt, which went around the waist. Of course, if you studied it and you put it on, you noticed it was here. You said, "Well, how the hell is it going to support me here (at the waist), when it should be here? (under the armpits)" There was snaps on the side. I tried it and it worked and I didn't inflate it, but a lot of fellows were playing with one another and firing the capsules off.

Of course, my name is Baldassari and it beings with BA. Everything in the service is done alphabetically. I was called down to the company clerk and he said, "You have bakery shop duty. You're in charge of the bakery shop detail. You'll report there at 4:00 in the morning. I said, "Where in the hell is the bake shop?" He said, "I don't know. You go find it." Well, we were down four or five decks, I don't remember. I came up under the main deck number one looking for the bake shop. Then I heard, "Oh, here comes bombs." They started with the bombing and returned fire. Then shouts of the men with their heads out of the portholes saying, "We got one. We got one. There it goes." Then the big explosion. Then everything went black and the smell of the explosion and you could hear screams and moans. I could see daylight ahead of me. I said, "I want to get to the daylight." In getting there, I was crawling over bodies, splintered wood. Finally I got to a steel ladder, because all of the wooden ladders had collapsed with the explosion. So I crawled up the steel ladder, because I knew there was a steel ladder behind the wood anyway. When I got to the main deck, there was an officer up there who said to me, "Sergeant, everyone out of that hole down below?" I said, "I didn't come from down below, but what's the problem?" He said, "I want to know if everybody is out." I said, "What do you want me to do about it?" He said, "Go down and find out if everyone is out of there." I went down the steel ladder, all the way down to the bottom. I didn't see anyone. It was dark. I asked, "Anyone down here?" No answer. So I went back up and I said, "There's no one down there, sir." "Okay."

Then I began to walk around, just size up what I was going to do. I said, "There's one thing I'm not going to do. I'm not going to panic. I'm going to take it cool and calm." The bomb came in on the port side, exploded down in the engine room and there was a great big gaping hole down on the port side. So I went down, I got around to that side and I find a friend of mine who finally became our first sergeant, pounding away at a hook which supported the skid that would deposit a large life raft in the water. At that time, they were also throwing these small life rafts, not looking at what was down in the water. They were bouncing them off the heads of survivors floating around in the water. So I said,

"Pat, what are you doing with that? You're not going to get that skid to go into the water." "I'll get it in the water," he said as he beat away. Finally he broke the chain, but it was rusted and painted to the skid and wouldn't slide into the water. So he said, "Well, I'm going over the side." I said, "Pat, don't go over the side, because it's not time to go. Stick with me. I'll tell you when to go." "No, no, I'm going." He slid down the rope and he didn't get to the water. He got short of the water and the eye that was woven into the end of the line went under his legs and hooked over his canteen belt. Now he's dangling on a line and he's rising and falling with the waves and his ass is whipping against the side of the ship and sizzling on the white hot plates. Well, I didn't see him. I said, "Pat, I told you not to go." I thought, "There's nothing I can do. I'm not going to pull him up. He wants out, well …" He told me later on that he had torn the hooks out of the web belt and freed himself and then floated over to the Clan Campbell with the life preserver.

Then I went on the other side of the ship and I met a couple of fellows that I knew from our outfit. The one we called Dutch wouldn't go over the side. He was standing in the corner of the bulkhead and the railing of the main deck. And he said if anyone came near him that he would beat them over the head with his rifle. He was not going over the side. I said, "Dutch, I only want to help you." "Get away from me," he said, "or I'll crack you in the head with my rifle." So I said, "If that's your wish, you got it." And he stayed aboard. I don't know what happened to him. I never saw him again.

Well, by that time, the ship had a pretty serious list on it. So I waited until the ship was flat in the water. The deck was level and the side of the ship then became the deck. I walked off the ship and into the water. I maybe jumped four or five feet into the water. That's how close I was to the water. I inflated my life belt, released the belt and got it up under my waist. At that point, I turned around and I saw a ship on the horizon. But it was 300-400 yards away. I said, "That's where I'm going." So I doggie paddled, kicked my legs and I gathered a group of men around me. I got into a large group and we began singing and saying, "Well, just like Coney Island." We finally managed to get to the Pioneer. We didn't know the name then, but I said, "Well, this looks like it's a destroyer. So we arrived at the port side of the vessel. They were attempting to climb a ladder that was on the stern of the port side. When I saw the ladder, I said, "That's odd. Why would there be a ladder here?" Then I realized maybe this is a minesweeper and that's to free the propellers of cables that become entangled in it.

The first man tried to go up and three or four men pulled him down. The second man tried, three or four men pulled him off. So I said, "This is crazy." I had about six men ahead of me. I said, "I'm not going to wait for this." I swam around to the starboard side, climbed up the ladder with no interference, got aboard the ship, relieved myself of my belt, and then I felt a chill. I said, "Boy." I was cold. By this time it was getting dark. So I found an entranceway mid-ship and I could hear and smell the engine room. I thought, "Oh, that's where I'm going, where there's heat." I went down and crawled atop the diesel engine, put my back up against the bulkhead and my butt on top of the diesel engine, dried out and got a little warmer, went upstairs, found the galley and looked for something to eat and drink. There was nothing, no coffee, no toast, no nothing. I said, "Well, at least I'm warm and I'm dry." So I took my wallet out and I took the money I had and I put it on the coffee urn, which was now empty, but it was heated by steam. I started to dry my money off and caught it as it fell down off the urn and I said, "This is mine, so I'm going to watch it." I put it back in my wallet and I went out on deck and I saw a line on the deck.

I saw they were tossing lines off to the men. So now I have no shoes, because my shoes came off my feet and I said, "Well, my shoes are gone.

I might just as well take the trousers off." So I dropped my trousers. I had no belt. I dropped the trousers and the fatigue jacket that was all that I had on me. Anyway, I got up aboard and in pulling so many men aboard, I lost my socks. I went right through the toes, so they became ankle socks. I pulled up maybe 30-35 men on the line. In doing so, I skinned both of my palms. This palm, of course, was very easy, the left hand which had been burned. But the right hand also skinned. So I'm bleeding. But at that point, the ship stopped picking up survivors. It stopped drifting. Then getting ahead and then drifting some more. I heard everybody say, "Oh, we're going back to shore. We were using a search light. I said, "Well, it's getting pretty late." But we turned around and we headed for Philippeville because we couldn't get any more men aboard the ship. That was the story the sailors were telling us. The captain wants us to take it back in because we can't take any more. How many we had aboard, I don't know.

Then an officer again came to me, one of my own officers, and he said, "Sergeant, there's a bunch of men on the back deck that they pulled up that were dead. I want you to go through the dog tags and see if any are from our outfit. I said, "But I don't have a flashlight. How am I going to tell?" These guys are piled up like cord wood. "Alright, Sarge, forget about it. When we get to shore, we'll check them out." So I didn't have to do that detail.

When we got to Philippeville, a little French fishing town with cobblestone streets. I can remember that. Now I'm barefooted, because I took the damn socks off. I was walking through these streets and the sisters from the Red Cross. What do they call them? Red Cross sisters. They were English. They gave us cigarettes and one of them said to me, "You're bleeding," because my hands were all bloody. She says, "You're bleeding." I wiped them on my shorts. She said, "Go over to that tent." So I went through that tent and they cleaned me up and put bandages on between my fingers and around the knuckles. As I went out of the tent, the guy said, "Give me your name, rank, and serial number." I told him, "Staff Sergeant Baldassari, 31st signal construction battalion." I gave my number, 325-68-475 and he flopped this box on the table and he said, "There's your purple heart." I said, "Thank you." Then he said, "Go up to that tent and they'll get your uniforms." We went up to the Canadian camp and they issued me a Canadian uniform, which on raw skin, it's wool, and it itched like hell and I can't stand wool. Well, I put the uniform on and the boots just to keep warm. I spent the day I think and then they said, "Oh, we're going to take you over to the American camp," where we got our own uniforms then.

Q: Okay. I want to back up just a little bit. I know it's just a small detail. You were talking about when you were in the water and you were singing songs. What songs were you singing?

Baldassari: Let me see now if I can remember. *Yes, we have no bananas, we have no bananas today* and there's one song about going up to the moon, coming down again. We sang that as we were going along. There was a group of us and we kept our spirits up singing. If you were to say to me, "Swim to that boat," I'd say, "I can't swim." But when they strafed us, I was Johnny Weissmuller. I kicked my feet and I was moving. We were just singing songs that were common and popular at that time. That's what we sang.

Q: Did you see the Rohna go down?

Baldassari: Oh yes. After I got away from the Rohna, before I gathered up with this bunch of guys, I turned around and said, "I want to see what's going on with the ship." At that time, the bow started to come up. Then she went "bbrrrmm" quickly she went down fast. Once it turned up, she went down. But it went down fast. I saw it go down.

Q: Did you lose any friends?

Baldassari: Oh yes. I lost a lot of friends. I thought at that time I'd lost Patterson. But when we got to the American camp, they started to come in from the Clan Campbell and all the other rescue vessels, the tugs and all and he showed up. His hair turned snow white. I said, "You got the sh-t scared out of you, didn't you?" He said, "I sure did!" I said, "Well, you didn't listen to me." He wouldn't admit it. He was that kind of a guy. He wouldn't admit it. But he got the sh-t scared out of him. He was sorry.

Q: I heard there was a roll call at some point where they tried to call off the names that they had and see who had survived.

Baldassari: Yes, we had a formation in the American camp. Of course, the call went out for all the 31st Signal survivors. They said, "31st Signal, report to this area". So we all went over and had a formation and they started to call names. That was sorry then. But all the survivors hadn't really come. A lot of them were in hospitals. There was one sergeant ... I think he was a tech sergeant. Yes, he was from down south and he was drifting out into the Atlantic when they picked him up. He spent 24 hours in the water. Recently I called him and I couldn't contact him, but I spoke to his nephew. I emailed him. His nephew worked in the news-paper and he had a computer available. So I emailed him and asked him if his cousin was coming to the reunion. The reply I got was that if he felt well, he was coming. I never saw him. He never made it.

Q: How old were you when you went in the service?

Baldassari: I was 21. I was turning 22 in December and I started in October. I was the youngest in the outfit. The only ones that were younger were the ones that were volunteers. I was a draftee. At that time, they were drafting 21s and 40s was the gap, because they had gone through the 24, 25, 26 and up. So it was 21 and 40. There were men in our outfit that were 40, 45 years old. But when we got the notice that we were the second army and they were going to send us on maneuvers overseas, they sent a lot of these 40 year old guys out of the Navy. They kept them in the States or they sent them home, because they considered them too old for active duty or overseas duty.

Q: Was there a difference between that young man that left for war and the one that came back? Did you change at all?

Baldassari: Did I change? Let me tell you, I appreciated life a lot more. I don't know how to explain it. I was a little more mature, I think, when I came back. I was raised during the Depression. I graduated from high school and I thought I was going to go to college. So my father said to me, "Well, you graduated. What do you want to do?" I said, "I'd like to go to college." He said, "I think you'd better get yourself a job so we can continue to eat." He was working at shipyards as a pipe fitter. Eventually, he got himself a steady job as a supervisor in the pipe fitting department. Then he hired me to come to work with him. Later I got the job as a printer in the newspaper. I started an apprenticeship at the newspaper in the composing room. I started at $12 a week.

Q: Is there anything else that you want to talk about on the Rohna? I'm kind of interested in you had gotten all those burns and all that. It was pretty fresh and you're dumped into the water.

Baldassari: My mother came from a fishing village and told me if they ever got a burn or something, they tended to treat it with saltwater. So that was in the back of my mind. Saltwater is nothing but the best thing for this. So when the Rohna got hit, the first thing that flashed through my mind, "Boy, it's going to be good for my hand, anyway."

We saw it. We saw the missile coming in, because a lot of the men that were assembled on the main deck, they milled around. There was an open hatch there that they could look out. Then there was a head to the right of that. They were hanging out around there. When they heard the fight going on and they saw the thing coming down, their heads were out the portholes watching. "Oh, we got one." When it went off, I don't know what happened to them. I assume that they got jammed into the opening, because wherever there's an opening, that's where the explosion's going to blow through. I never knew what happened. That deck was strewn with bodies. Because they made a troop carrier out of the ship, they lined all the holds. They covered the holds with planking. Not the covers, but regular planking. The floors and everything was wood lined. They didn't have bunks, they had hammocks. They slung the hammocks over the tables that you were assigned to eat your meals. You slung your hammocks over that. So there was a lot of wood in the place. That wood, when it exploded, became missiles. Some of the guys had 4 x 4s, 2 x 4s through their bodies. Blood, the deck was so slippery; it was very hard to stand on. There were so many guys bleeding and moaning. The most frequent plea was "momma, momma, momma." They were all young kids. That's all you heard was "momma." It was touching. It got to you. I don't know how I would have reacted. It was something. You never forget it, though. I remember I went to see *The Titanic.* That last scene where there's that moan and you see all the bodies in the water, all the people in the water. That last moan, that's the way it was when the Rohna went down. That moan and the cry. I suppose it was the guys that were dying. They were calling "momma." It's funny the way the first thing they do is call for their mothers.

Q: A lot of the guys have mentioned that sound. You said you saw the missile hit?

Baldassari: Well, I saw it coming this way before it turned. It went by the Rohna and then turned around and came in and hit her in the port side. It was flaming from the back and the cry went up, "We got one! We got one!" But it wasn't. It got us. We had two attacks. They came first and then it dropped off. The sound of the fighting dropped off and then they came back again. That's when they hit us. They got us then when they came back the second time. We had air cover before they came in. They came out of the sun. They came out of France, turned around and came out. They came from the north, went to the south and then flew out of the sun and got us. They got us.

AN INTERVIEW WITH STANLEY COHEN
Rohna Survivor

Edited for readability

Cohen: I originally was with the 323rd Fighter Control Squadron and when the 322nd got ready to go overseas they were ten men short. In order to fill the cadre they took ten people from the 323rd, which wasn't going to be going overseas until about maybe two months from then and they moved them up to the 322nd. That is how I got to be with the 322nd.

When the ship was hit all chaos broke out, a type of chaos that you can't describe. You have to be there. We for example had one man in our outfit, he went into a corner, and finally we said to him, we got to get off of here. Come on. He said I am not going. We said come on, we'll help you. Come on. We went over near him and he was like a tiger. He was ready to kill us, and we had to leave him alone.

I initially was up in the top deck and there were some lifeboats there and there were two or three people besides myself. We decided to get into the lifeboat after we knew that we had to abandon ship, although we never really ever got any order to abandon ship and from what I understand nobody else did either. We got into the boat and we started to lower it. And as we lowered it from the deck we were on to the one below, a mass of GIs came rushing to get onto the boat. And I said this is not for me. There was just absolute chaos.

So I jumped off the boat. As I was going away from the boat, I turned to look to see what was happening and a lot of GIs were piling into the boat and it couldn't stand the weight. The cables were weak, and one end just collapsed and fell and spilled all of those who were in it quite a distance into the Mediterranean Sea and I doubt that anybody in that boat survived. After going on deck and seeing some of my mates including the one who I said was in a corner (we never got him off), I went onto the deck. And at that point there was a captain standing there and saying, "The Germans are going to come back and they are going to strafe. Put on your helmets." And a lot of the men were putting on their helmets. Along came a PFC who pushed the captain aside and said, "You damn fool. You are killing them." When they put on their helmets with the strap under their chin, at this point in time the ship was listing, so the rope ladders over the side were above the water maybe 15–20 feet. So when you got down the ladder, you had to drop 15 or 20 feet. This meant the water would rush under the helmet and snap your neck, so the PFC was quite knowledgeable and so he was then telling everybody who was about go over the rail to get rid of your helmets. In the meantime myself and a couple of others went rushing to the rail and started screaming at those who were going down the ladder to get rid of your helmets. It'll kill you when you hit water and I guess we saved quite a few lives by getting those people on the net to throw away their helmets.

While I was still on the deck we had some of these life craft. They were like skids and all you had to do theoretically was to go to the wall, get a hatchet, knock the pin out and it would go shooting out into the water in order to have some place for people to get on and stay afloat.

I got that axe and banged at that pin with all my might for probably 30 seconds or a minute and it wouldn't budge. It was rusted. It was like it was welded. It was impossible to get that pin out. It was all one piece.

I then started to go over the side and down the rope ladder and I remember saying to myself, "This can't be happening to me, not to me, can't happen, can't happen". And as I got to the bottom, I let go of the rope, I fell the 15-20 feet and the water was cold and I said, "Holy cow! What's happening to me?" I was wearing a life preserver, which I had inflated. We were never given any instructions about the life preserver. We had two evacuation drills at which time we were told nothing, just to stand there and that was it. I was wearing the life preserver, which had two tubes around my waist and I squeezed the two places where the CO_2 tubes were and the life preserver expanded and was operable and I was wearing it around my waist. I got into the water and I started to try to swim as best I could. I am not a swimmer and never knew really how to swim and I found that I was swallowing a lot of water. What was happening, by wearing the life preserver around my waist instead of under my arms where I should have, my rear end was sticking up high, forcing my head and my feet into the water. If I had been instructed properly, I would have been wearing it under my armpits and therefore my upper body would have been above the water. I started to swallow a lot of water and I said this can't go on. And I decided I would flip over on my back and use my hands as oars. My upper body was up and so my head was out of the water, because of the movement of my shoulders, my waist and my upper body was out of the water, which was fine.

I then remembered that the first thing to do was get away from the boat, because when the boat sinks there is a pull like a vacuum and pulls as it goes down. I kept saying to myself "keep calm, keep cool, get away from the boat", and using my hands as oars I got away from the boat. The ship was a blazing inferno at this point and there was no doubt it was going to sink. I tried to stay away from anybody at this point, because somebody might be in trouble and come over and try to latch on to me and pull me down. So I felt the best thing to do with all of this chaos, I was better off being a lone person.

At the point where I felt I was far enough away, I turned around to see what was in store for me. And I looked to see if there were any boats in the area. There were no people and no boats in the area. I didn't know what would become of me. This must have gone on for about 10 or 15 minutes and I was right in the middle of the Mediterranean all by myself.

Finally I caught a glimpse of a boat coming around from the distance. Later I found out it was circling the area. And as it cut close enough I decided to swim out and try to intercept it. I finally got to the side of the boat, which was the Pioneer, and I figured I would just scamper up the rope ladder. I grabbed a hold of it with my right arm and held on and then my left arm before I could get it up to the next rung it was like eternity, because I had very little power. I didn't realize that I was so exhausted. And so then I went up with the right arm and then I went up with the left arm, which seemed like an eternity when one of Indian crew decided that I wasn't going up fast enough, so he tried to climb over me and push me off so he could get up to the railing of the ship a little faster. He didn't like how slow I was going and I had no alternative because I was exhausted. Fortunately I have sharp elbows and I gave him one poke with my elbow and he went flying back into the water so that he was then in a position to then catch a bottom rung while I was going up to the top. It's just, at that point it is life preserving. You do things that you certainly wouldn't normally do, but there is such a strong impulse even when I was alone in the water, it is stay cool, stay calm and you will be okay. I finally got close to the top rung and two big hands grabbed my wrists and dragged me up like a wet rag onto the deck and never was a deck a happier place to be. During the course of the voyage they had to move the men around from one side of the boat to the other side of the boat, because the mere massive weight of the survivors was tipping the boat. And in order not to capsize it, they had to start to distribute the weight. Then I think something like one o'clock in the morning when they had about a little over 600 survivors, they headed for Philippeville and that is where we eventually wound up.

Q: How long do you think you were in the water?

Cohen: Well you know you don't look at your watch while you are swimming. As best as I could imagine it probably was somewhere between an hour and an hour and a half, and the sea, there were 20 foot swells. It was an absolute exhausting situation. The crew of the Pioneer they broke out their lockers. They took off our wet clothes. They distributed whatever they had. They were absolutely magnificent.

Q: Tell me a little bit about where you were on the Rohna when things happened and what was going on around you. This was before the bomb hit and then lead me through when the bomb hit and then how you get up on deck.

Cohen: We were in a position before the bomb hit, I think in pretty good position, because I understand a lot of people were way down in the lower decks. We were fairly high in the decks and we were looking out of portholes and watching a couple of the dog fights between some of the French and British aircraft and the Germans and that was going on all afternoon. And it was the last bomber after the others had gone by and we were watching some of the German bombers being hit by anti-aircraft and by the defending aircraft go in flames down and it was quite exciting, just watching actual dog fights.

Q: How did you know the bomb hit? Some people were close and some weren't.

Cohen: You felt the bomb hit. I mean we were hit. I never heard a command to abandon ship nor do I think anybody else did. Absolute chaos broke out. We didn't know how to wear our life preservers. We didn't know to try to get into a boat or not to try to get into a boat, wear our helmets, not helmets. I observed this one poor sap. He had on his Eisenhower jacket. He loaded it up with C-rations, what the hell he was going to eat. He put on his helmet. He put on a full backpack, his rifle, went to the side of the boat and jumped into the water. He went down and we never saw him again. So when you are in a situation where all chaos is breaking loose and it did as soon as we were hit and all of these strange things happening, the only thing I kept saying is, "keep cool, keep calm, get away from the chaos because that is going to do you in", and the fact that I got out of that lifeboat saved my life. And everything I did, thank God, that day I kept my wits about me and I survived.

Q: Have you had the opportunity to share this story over the years?

Cohen: I am a little different than I think most people that I heard today in that I was so thrilled that I was alive that I wanted people to know. I wanted people to know; now this is not right after the war, because right after the war it was a very deep secret. But after I got back home there was no need of secrecy any more. And so I did, I told my family and I told what happened and just as I am telling you, because it was a wonderful story. Not wonderful that all of those people were killed, but that I, not knowing how to swim was still able to survive to be a survivor from these kinds of circumstances. I was proud of myself and sorry for all the others.

A story connected with this perhaps sometime in the 80s, my wife and I went to a tour of France. We started in Paris and we went all the way down to the south coast to Cannes, and we saw many of the stops in between. It was a wonderful, wonderful trip. We always enjoyed Paris and if we went anywhere else in Europe we'd always leave from Paris, spend a couple of days there, because that was the dessert. When we got down further south in Cannes, the tour had chosen the Carlton, which is one of the elite hotels. I had a room that faced the magnificent Cannes beach where the women would sun their entire bodies. It was just a beautiful sight and I went to the window knowing what I was about to see and my wife came running over to me. What's the matter? I had burst into tears and I said this isn't beautiful. This is the sea of death. There are 1,100 of my fellow soldiers dead in that sea and I was uncontrollable. It certainly has had a very big impact on my life.

I never knew the group that we were with today existed until last September when I was with a dentist who happens to be a history buff and he knew all about the Arizona and Pearl Harbor and he said you lost more people than they did on the Arizona. There must be something on the Internet. And the next day I got a 50 page fax from him, which listed all of the people who were killed and all the survivors. And then I looked down the list of survivors and I saw my name and I shook for about five or ten minutes. It was just an unbelievable feeling that of all of those people I survived.

Q: Did this change your life at all?

Cohen: It changed my life to the effect that I guess I was just happy that I survived. Of all of the people that were on that boat we saved 800 and we lost about 1,100. I don't know how to swim. I was alive. I was thankful to God that I had made it. And to this day, I am thankful to God that here I am so many years later and having gone through a heart attack in 1966, a by-pass surgery in 2004, lung cancer in 1999 where I lost the upper lobe of my right lung and all of the cancer, I am still here after all of these years after everything that I have gone through. And I have a wonderful wife of some 60 odd years. I have three wonderful children and two wonderful grandchildren and one of my children is right here in the room with me. He came along to just take care of me since it is a little more difficult now for me to get around and I am ever grateful to him. And to life and my business world things were very rough. I came from a poor family. They gave me nothing except love and I had the best parents anybody could ever have. And in my business affairs, in 1983 I almost lost everything and then after that the flower opened up. So I am a very, very fortunate person in many respects. I have enough to take care of me and my wife and my grandchildren and my children. And I am just, at this point, I am enjoying life, enjoying my children, enjoying my wife, enjoying my grandchildren and very thankful I am here today.

AN INTERVIEW WITH ROBERT DANKERT
Rohna Survivor

Edited for readability

Q: I just really want you to tell your story as to what happened on the Rohna. I'll start with how you got into the military and what led up to you heading towards the Rohna.

Dankert: Well, I was drafted and went to Fort Niagara. That was where I was inducted. I can't think of the name of the camp where we had basic. From there, we went to Dyersburg, Tennessee, next to Mobile, Alabama and then shipped out of Newport News, Virginia. On the Liberty ship we had two meals a day. Breakfast was oatmeal, which was wormy. We discovered them and the guy was picking them out. Of course, after a couple of days, you didn't bother about picking out the meal worms. They wouldn't hurt you anyway. We were around 30 days, I think it was, or close to it across the Atlantic and landed in Oran, Africa. From there, I think we went up, I think it was on Lion Mountain. It was nothing but a rock pile and set up a tent. You couldn't drive a stake anywhere. So we picked up rocks and tied the tent to the rocks. We were there I can't tell you just how long, but we worked on sort of a building for supplies. It was next to a prisoner of war camp with Italians.

Q: What did you think of the Rohna when you first saw it?

Dankert: It was something different, I'll tell you, in my estimation. Of course, we weren't on it long enough to really know too much about it. It was an old, old ship. The fellow that I was with, we were down in the hold in the old dining hall, which at that time years back when it was a newer ship. They gave us hammocks. That's where we slept in the hammocks at night and rolled them up and then the tables were still left. The eats weren't too damn good. I remember we first had biscuits. They opened them up and I never saw anything like it before. Apparently, there was bug's eggs in it and the heat from baking them hatched them and bugs came out.

I was out on deck and it was drawing towards evening. We see these planes in the air and I see this bomber and I see a couple of fighter planes, one coming each way at it. All of a sudden, there's smoke coming from behind the bomber, and down he went. This was quite a way's off, more or less. It wasn't long and everybody was sent below deck. So I went down below deck. I had a buddy who was talking and then there was quite a lot of racket of guns. I guess they had guns above deck. All of a sudden the bomb hit, there was like all hell, even the air, the dust even burnt your skin. I had put on my steel helmet and it blew it off. The buddy of mine, he was standing next to me and his face was bleeding. Something hit him. Before this happened, the sea was quite rough. There were portholes on the Rohna and I stuck my head out one of them. We were stern far enough, so you could see one of the big propellers every now and then. It would come out of the water. Anyway, after this explosion, everything was black. Lights, everything went off. There was a big stairway that went from one deck to another. The explosion blew that down. We had to set that up to get out. Next to where we were standing is the loading holes on the ship where they load a ship. I don't know if you know what I'm speaking of, but they go one above the other. They're covered up with a big heavy plank. There was a bunch of guys sitting on that platform when the bomb it. The next second, they were gone. You could see sky right up through. It took out every one of the hatch covers.

Q: Did you see the bomb?

Dankert: No. Me and a buddy of mine, he didn't make it. We started up, set the stairway up and there were barracks bags everywhere, fire jumping from one barracks bag to another. One of the soldiers was laying there. He was hurt bad. A buddy of mine got on one side and I was on the other and we had to really drag him. We stood him up on deck and they took care of him. What happened to him, I have no idea. Then his buddy, he said he was going to try to find a rope or something to drop down into the hold. There were fellows way down in the ship, but there was nothing you could do. There was no way of getting to them. But he was going to see if he could find them. That's the last I'd see of him.

By that time, the ship was listing pretty good. I went towards the bow and then I came back on the high side where the bomb went in. Here's the steel, it's about ¾ of an thick or whatever. A big chunk of it laid straight out right underneath two lifeboats, which never got lowered because there was no way to lower them. I went toward the stern and there was a lifeboat. It was loaded, which we were told never to do that. You lower the lifeboat and then you go down and get into it. Here they had loaded it and I thought, "Oh, my god." You know what happened? The one guy manning the rope on one end, he threw it too fast and it just tipped up and they go out like cord wood. So I said, "It's time I'm getting off." So I went over to the rail. I guess it was forward of where the bomb went in. By that time, the ship was a long way to the water. But they always told us to get off the high side. So that's what I did. I went over the rail. There was a rope hanging down. So I got hold of that. As

I'm going down, the side of the ship was pretty hot. It was almost like the soles of my shoes were smoking a little. I get down a ways and no more rope. I look down and it's a long ways yet; and I let go. I didn't know if I was going to come back up or not. I was ready to suck in some water. But I did get back up before I did. I guess my life preserver was working okay.

Q: Had you inflated that before you went in the water?

Dankert: Yes. I said, "I'm going to swim away from the ship before it goes down and I get sucked in with it." Then I ran into another buddy of mine from Company C, a young fellow. Of course, we were all young. Him and I teamed up and we started and along comes one of the lifeboats and it was loaded. When we got near them, they just went nuts. "Stay away! Stay away!" There was no way I was even going to get anywhere near it. I thought it was about ready to sink anyway. But it was loaded. Then we saw the minesweeper and started swimming towards it. Before I really knew it, more or less, we were there. But anyway, I got to the side of it and I see a hand bar welded to the side of it and I grabbed hold of that. The next thing I knew, I'm hanging up in mid-air. Luckily, the right side of it was a rope ladder with wood steps on it, right next to it. I was at about the last round of it. I couldn't pull myself up. No way. Here, I'm hanging in the air and all of a sudden, a swell comes and I go way up where I can get my feet in the bottom of it. I climbed up and a sailor helped me over the rail and took me around near the engine room, because when they started up, it really vibrated.

Then we landed in port (Philippeville, Algeria) and ended up in an English camp. I guess probably some of the others did, too. Well, I know they did. They gave us English uniforms. In the middle of camp was a cast iron thing with tea. I remember that. I was there a while and got on what they call the 40 and 8 railroad. I went from there and I can't remember the name of the camp where we ended up. We went over the mountains. We camped in an orchard.

Q: How many close buddies do you think you lost that day?

Dankert: Quite a few. Schneider was really the closest to me. He was designated as carpenter. He and I were both carpenters. We got along good. He was from Danbury, Connecticut.

Q: Your own life, did this event make major changes?

Dankert: I don't know. I can't really tell you. We never talked much about it, anyway. It definitely made you think. It bothered you sleeping, but I guess it did that with everybody. I guess everybody is thankful it seemed like things worked. You thought for the worst. Some things they seem like it's for the worse and it comes out better.

Q: When you dropped into the water, you said you went down quite a ways.

Dankert: Yes.

Q: That must have been a time that you thought, "Maybe I won't make it."

Dankert: Yes, that's right. What I'll never forget is the swells were so big. There were no breakers or anything, but the swells were awful big. When I went down into the low part of the swell, I swore that I was going to be drowned. Everywhere you looked was water. You looked up and there was water way up over your head. But you just float up with it. You never forget that, though. In the water like that, and then one of those big transports goes by you. You'll never see anything so big in all your life.

Q: How long do you think you were in the water?

Dankert: I really can't tell you; probably a couple of hours. I know it was dark. We never talked too much about it. I guess there's been more talk about it after the reunions started and all this and that. I think probably if you talk to a lot of the others, it's probably been the same thing. I don't know why. Who cares about it anyway?

AN INTERVIEW WITH STANLEY HILL

Rohna Survivor

Edited for readability

Hill: I was one of the youngest survivors on the Rohna. I found out that by eight months, I was younger than the other guy. Raised up in Oklahoma, went in the service early 1942 and had my basic at Jefferson Barracks, shipped me out from there to Miami Beach and I took a battery of tests and passed it for the Army Air Corps. I was glad to get out of the grunts, the infantry and went into the Army Air Corps, got to Miami Beach, we moved the civilians out of the hotels and we moved in. It was a small detachment there then.

When I reported in I had made acting PFC to escort these troops down on the troop train. And this second Lieutenant asked me, he said "Are you in charge?" I said, yes I was. And he said, "Well what type of training have you had?" I said I have had infantry basic at Jefferson Barracks. He takes right out on there and said, okay you will be a drill instructor here starting two days from now. I will give you a couple of days to get acclimated to the weather. So I stayed there for eight and a half months, putting guys through basic and that was the start of my military career.

Well when I met a friend of mine from my same hometown out of Oklahoma and by this time I had made buck sergeant. I was going up fast compared to some of the other boys, because they had been in a couple of years and they were still corporals. And he said, "Why don't you turn casual down here and we will sign up for overseas and get a little action," both young, 18 years old. And I said "okay I will do that." So I went in the orderly room and told this field sergeant, I said, "How do I turn casual?" He said, "Why?" I said, "I want to get where the action is." He said, "Okay sign these papers." I signed the papers. A couple of days I had my orders going to Bradley Field, Connecticut and I was placed in the 322nd Fighter Control Squadron.

When I reported in up there, Sergeant Ekiss the first sergeant, he looked at me. I was standing at the desk out there reporting in to the chief clerk. He said, "Where did you come from?" I said, "Miami Beach." He said, "You have one hell of a tan." I said, "Well I have been down there eight months." He said, "Are you in pretty good physical condition?" I said, "Excellent." There was nothing I couldn't do (or I wouldn't admit). He said, "Can you perform calisthenics?" I said, "Yes I can." He said, "Okay, 0600 tomorrow morning out in front of the barracks, *calahoopics*". I wanted to correct him. I thought no, you better wait because he was the first sergeant. And I said, "I will be there." So 6 o'clock the next morning I was out there. So I performed calisthenics for the 322nd until we left to go overseas. And I was in the training then, I figured it out then, to be a first sergeant. I was under his command and that is what I eventually turned out to be, the first sergeant, and that is why I retired as a chief master sergeant. You couldn't get any higher in the enlisted ranks. I had made them all. And that is how I wound up in the 322nd.

Next we went down to Newport News, Virginia and it reminded me of a concentration camp of what I read in the paper. They had barbed wire all around, locking gates. And I thought no, this is not for me. I was like a caged animal inside that because I was raised on the farm, come and go as you wanted to. But we stayed there I think six days if I am not mistaken. And they loaded us on the USS Nicholas Gilman going to North Africa. We didn't really know, but we had a good idea we were headed for North Africa, Rock of Gibraltar, which that proved to be true. And we arrived near Oran and unloaded and lived in tents oh I guess maybe two or three weeks. And then we met a convoy coming from Ireland and that is when they put us on the Rohna.

The Rohna looked like a rusty tub of bolts when I first saw it. I told some of my buddies, I said, "We will be very fortunate if we make this trip on this tub." And sure enough it proved that we didn't make it. When I was on the Rohna I had duty as sergeant of the guard from midnight till six in the morning. We were down in the second hold down below. I would volunteer to get out of there to do anything to get out of that hole. And as long as I was sergeant of the guard I could smoke my cigarettes in private and get back behind with the blanket over our head. I could do that where the other guys couldn't. And I would come off duty 6 o'clock in the morning, and we were on deck when the dog fight started.

Q: It started about six?

Hill: No. I was in a dice game. We shot dice, played cards or whatever. It didn't actually start until a little after three in the afternoon, but I was still there with my boys. We were shooting, playing a little dice game going. And when it started, that is the first action we had seen. So I was on deck and I watched it from the deck. Had my shoes, gas mask, helmet, 45, had everything all neatly stacked over by the bulkhead where I came out of the hold of the ship. My buddy Leo, he was taking odds. He was pretty smart. He was a city boy from Dorchester, Mass and I was an old country boy from Oklahoma and I could rattle the dice pretty good and he was excellent in taking bets. And he was handling the money and I was shooting the dice. We had a good game going. We stayed there and watched the dog fight. And then we saw, it looked like a toy aircraft release and it circled around. And I told him, I said "That dude is going to hit us." Sure enough it did, hit us at the waterline, knocked the engine out the other side.

So, guys were screaming, hollering. I never saw my first sergeant after that. But up until then we had been pretty close on the ship. We would coordinate things together because me being sergeant of the guard, he wanted to know everything that happened. And I had to fill out a report and give it to him.

But when Dick, when Sergeant Ekiss went down in the hold, I understand we had one guy in confinement, locked up in the stockade down below. Sergeant Ekiss went down to relieve the man and he got him out. And when the sergeant was coming back up I guess the whole thing exploded and that is when he was killed. The prisoner went on to China with us, not under confinement. He went over as a buck private and he turned out to be a sad alcoholic. He was absolutely worthless.

I was in the water about eight hours after I left the ship. I wasn't really that scared. I guess I was too ignorant to be scared. I knew I was a good swimmer and I was in excellent physical condition, so I figured well I will just swim to shore. But what I got a little confused of which way shore was. But Leo Kelly, the friend of mine, he was in the water with me. He had on a wool turtleneck sweater. After we got in the water he said, "Stan I can't swim. My sweater is wool, absorbing so much water I got to get rid of it." We had a hatch cover that we were holding on to. We got the turtleneck sweater off of him and we got his fatigue jacket back on, and from that time on we hung on to the hatch cover. But my hand, this hand here was completely … I couldn't move my fingers at all. I didn't know what was wrong. It just looked like it was a crystal where the salt water had just corroded the whole thing. Had it not been for that in the salt water, I would probably have bled to death. I could use my thumb. And I told him, I said, "I can't move my fingers." He said, "I am not hurt." And I said, "You're not?" "Nothing, no I am not hurt." Well later on, after we got to land, he had a piece of shrapnel in his shoulder about an inch and a half long that was just stuck in there and he had bled quite a bit on his fatigues and the salt water had closed the gap you know.

So after about, I would say close to a little over eight hours that we was in the water, the Pioneer picked us up, USS Pioneer, the minesweeper. And when I got on, I think it was Jones that picked me up, the little red headed bosun and he said, "Are you hurt?" I said, "Yeah, I got something wrong with my hand." He looked at it. They laid me on the table inside the galley. He said, "Well we have no more anesthetic." He said, "But we have a little rum." I said, "Good." He was pouring it out in a cup and I said, "A little bit more." So he poured a little more in and I drank that and they sewed up my hand, did a beautiful job. I can use my fingers, no problem. Leo, he was standing up there and he said, "Well dig this thing out of mine." So they took this piece of shrapnel out of him. I guess when the ship exploded stuff just went every place, because I found out later on I had a couple of pieces in my leg that I had removed in the military later on, little pieces came up and they were sore and the doctor dug them out and it was metal, so it must have come off of the Rohna, because that was the only other place that I had been.

We dropped off in Philippeville, North Africa with the rest of the troops. We was issued British uniforms to get rid of our wet clothes and I wore that British uniform for about four or five days until we got to an American rest camp and they supplied us with the uniforms. And our

Commander said, "Okay we are going on to China, Burma and India." Good deal, we've already been in a little combat, let's hit it. So I guess it's probably 50 of us that survived out of my unit, out of the 322nd and we hung together then the rest of the war. But we were split up once we hit China. We were split up and went all over. I was all over China, which wasn't really that bad looking back, but it seems like a dream to me now after all those years. That was in 1944 and 1945, so, I survived it, lived through it.

Q: Take me back to the actual Rohna itself. Is there any other description of what was going on up on deck?

Hill: The dog fights, yeah. The first thing I heard was the ack ack off of the ships and I, of course they had the sirens going first and I heard that. Well we knew then something was under attack. And when the planes first appeared, I looked up and I saw some P-47 fighters and I said, "Those are our fighters." And Leo said, "Yeah, but those are not our bombers." And I looked over, well here was these German bombers coming in, probably maybe 25, I don't know how many it was, but it looked like about three flights, maybe seven planes in a flight, so from that I would say at least 20 to 25 planes. And they stayed around for well over an hour trying to hit our ships and we were zigzagging and the planes were dog fighting. Some of them shot some down. Some of our ships shot some of the bombers down. I seen them, you know I could see them fall, and we made no attempt to pick up the survivors of the aircraft. And I saw a couple of our fighters go down. And I would say after about 35 or 40 minutes under attack, that is when they started to leave and it ceased off just for a little bit and here came two or three other planes and that was the one that was carrying the toy. I saw this lone plane standing off by itself and it was quite a little ways off. And of course on deck it was a lot of people hollering and you know people were actually crying, scared you know, first time under attack. But I was more curious than I was scared up until then. And I kept looking at this plane and when he released that aerial torpedo, radio control it looked like a toy aircraft. It wasn't too long and length wasn't too wide, and I figured, well that was like a hand control job you know, and then it more or less circled around and then zeroed in on the Rohna. I knew then it was coming our way.

Now some of our guys were below deck and they were telling me that they were looking through the portholes. And when the concussion went off, one guy, his head was stuck in the porthole and I guess you know it killed him like that. But you hear a lot of stories from the guys depending on where on the ship they were. And I didn't wait around too long after that ship was hit, because I knew I wanted to get off and I knew it was going to sink, and I didn't go off the high side. I went off the low side.

But even today it seems like a clouded dream. You know it just doesn't really seem real. And for all those years, in the military I might have told ten people. I didn't talk about it. I put it on the back burner. I was asked a few times by the orderly room personnel that kept our records, how and when did I receive the Purple Heart, and I was a little sarcastic at the time I would answer. I would say "Now where do you think I got it? Do you think I was playing jacks? Do you think I was playing snooker?" And I really didn't give them an answer except one Commander that I had. He sat me down and he said, "I want to know where you got it, when you got it, what the action was," and I told him, and I could hardly talk. He said, "Why don't you talk about it?" I said, "Do you understand what I went through?" He said, "Well I was in combat." I said, "Did you ever leave a sinking ship?" He said, "No." I said, "Then you wouldn't understand a word I'm talking about. You don't have the feeling that I have." I did confide in my wife. I told her. I have three girls. My oldest one, she knew about it. The other two didn't.

Up until right before the San Antonio reunion, we were having Thanksgiving dinner in Palm Springs with my daughter who has a condo down there. Every Thanksgiving after I had returned from overseas, I would always say, "Well today is a good day and it is also a bad day." And finally my youngest daughter said, "Dad why do you always say that?" I said, "Well it's a good day that I am alive. It's a bad day, because I had to swim the Mediterranean." She said, "Well what did you swim the Mediterranean for?" And I told her. Well my middle daughter picked up and she said, "I am going to get on the Internet right now and I am going to find out about the Rohna." She did and here was, came up 15 or 20 pages about the Rohna. She says, "Dad you are going to the reunion at San Antonio and we are going to take you."

But I didn't want to talk about it, and the other survivors, very few of them talked about it. I couldn't talk about it to someone who had not been there. But now with the survivors that we've all got it out of our system, it is easy to talk about it. And now my kids all the time they say, "Tell me some more Dad. What about this". So they have made videos like Mike's doing. They've got it all on tape. Now they are putting it on DVD. And I told them, I said "Well somebody has to tell the story." So they have it.

I was called to Washington, DC. A Congressman from Orange County wanted to interview me. I had a granddaughter that was in politics and she got me up there. This was two years ago, and Congressman Royce interviewed me and his dad who was also a combat man out of Europe. He had received the Purple Heart with two clusters, and we had a General sitting between us and we were interviewed. I got back to Orange County, he showed this at his little briefing in Orange County every Saturday. Well I got some calls. "Thought you were dead." I said, "No I am still alive." But some of the people I didn't even know called me up and told me and said, "Hey I saw you on TV." It was a local TV. I said, "No I am still alive." But it was something really personal and I just didn't want to talk about it until I got to the reunion and then, like my wife said, "Now we can't shut you up Stan". I said, "Yeah, that's right." But this reunion means a lot to me.

Q: Well is there anything left that you haven't told anyone yet?

Hill: No, well some of the things I did that I will never tell, in China. We won't go into that. But all my buddies down here, they remind me. We just learned to survive. But some of the other things that I wouldn't tell Mike, I wouldn't tell you or I haven't told my wife or anybody else. But these boys that I meet with once a year, they keep reminding me of little things, and I guess we will just keep it among ourselves.

Q: I just have a quick question. You mentioned that there was a prisoner down below. You didn't mention his name. Do you know his name?

Hill: Fitzgerald. Black hair, Irish man, had a black mustache, smoked English cigarettes. He was really a lush. He was a lush in the States. I knew him in the States and then especially after we got to China. He didn't even go to work. He was a lush. We sent him back to the States, absolutely worthless. Then we had another boy there who, I don't know how he got on the wrong foot, but he got caught selling cigarettes and he got ten or 12 years in Leavenworth. He was a corporal. And he had worked for me some, but I can't remember his name, but they court-martialed him, general court-martial and sent him back to Leavenworth.

When I joined, I was only 18; I was 19 when this all happened, and it was a great life. My military life was one of the best. That was one I was really proud of. I started at the bottom and worked right to the top.

AN INTERVIEW WITH CARLTON JACKSON

Author of "Allied Secret: The Sinking of HMT Rohna"

Edited for readability

Q: How did you first become interested in the Rohna?

Jackson: Well, I teach U.S. Social History, for one thing, and I'm also a former newspaper reporter. I used to work for the Birmingham Post Herald when I was a student at Birmingham Southern, and any talent I have for writing I learned from being a newspaper reporter. I get a lot of ideas about books and articles simply by reading the newspaper. Well, one day in November of 1993, I picked up the Sunday paper and I noticed a little column called "Today in History" and it mentioned the Rohna as being the greatest loss of

life at sea during World War II. And the article mentioned John Fievet, from Birmingham, Alabama. Well, the next day in my office, I called Directory Assistance and five minutes later, I was talking with John Fievet, and it turns out that he and I both are graduates of Birmingham Southern College, which is probably the best liberal arts college in the country, and so we hit it off right away. I went over to his house. He helped me compile a list of survivors who were living at that time. I began to write letters and in the course of time, I received well over a hundred letters from survivors who not only encouraged me to do the project, but were very pleased that someone was doing the project, because they felt, as I did, that it was long overdue, that these people got proper recognition. That's how it started.

Q: Then you began your research?

Jackson: I began the research as I've just mentioned, plus the letters and telephone calls and tape recordings from the survivors, and from friends of survivors and family members, and the like. Then there were many records at the National Archives in Washington, which I went through rather carefully. Also, there were records at the Public Records Office in Kew, London. Today, that's called the National Archives of England. They had several folders dealing with KMF-26, the name of the convoy in which the Rohna was traveling, and the like. So I went to Kew the first time about 1994 and spent quite a bit of time. It was like looking for the proverbial needle in a haystack because I would literally page through these thick volumes of material until I came to something relating to KMF-26 or the Rohna or any of the escort ships. I found some information on the Banfora, the Egra and the Pioneer, (one of the few American ships in that vicinity). I ultimately wound up getting quite a bit of information from the PRO in London. Then, I came back to Western Kentucky University and set about trying to find any members of the German plane from which the fatal missile was fired.

I wrote to a friend of mine at the Smithsonian Institution in Washington, and asked him for suggestions. He told me I should saturate all of the Veterans' groups in Germany with letters, in German. As bad as my German is, he strongly recommended that I do them *auf Deutsch* rather than in English. And I did; bad German and all. I wrote about twenty letters to every Veterans' organization I could find. About a month later, I received a letter from the Veterans' group in Bonn, Germany, telling me that not only did they know the name of the pilot who flew the Heinkle 177 that fired the Henschel 293 rocket at the Rohna, but they had just spoken with him. And so they gave me his telephone number and I telephoned him immediately and we had a long conversation. He was Major Hans Dochtermann, and I went over to see him in October of 1995. I spent a day at his home, interviewing him for this book. He sent me written material, again, in German, and I translated as well as I could, but I did have the services of an expert in the German language to double-check me to make sure that I was getting it right. I think putting the Major into the book gave it more of an international perspective than it would have had otherwise if I had never come across it. And, as I understand, he has two grandsons and a son living in the United States. I've never meet either any of them but I did get a letter from his grandson, Shawn. He is a fisherman in Kodiak, Alaska. I let John Fievet know about it and he, in turn, let other members of the Association know about it. And, as I understand, Major Dochtermann's son was at your meeting in Seattle, Washington a few years ago, which I did not attend. But I would love to meet him.

Q: Tell me about Major Dochtermann.

Jackson: He died in 1999, about four years after I had met him. But he was very gracious to me, he and his; I assume it was his wife. She fixed a very good lunch for us. He had little model airplanes suspended from the ceiling of his living room. He said that he deeply regretted the damages that he had caused, but he was, he said, a frontline soldier who had taken an oath of allegiance to the Third Reich, in the way that GIs always take an oath to the American Constitution. But there's always this feeling of remorse that you were responsible for so much pain and suffering.

Q: Did he mention any other successful missions?

Jackson: He was a part of the Blitz, in London, at the beginning of the war. This is in late 1940, and on into '41, when the Blitz was happening. I think I'm right on those dates. And he was over Germany. Then after the Rohna, he was on the Russian front for a time. At the end of the war, he was taken prisoner by the British, and he was held for a time at Stratford-on-Avon. I don't know if he saw any Shakespeare plays while he was there <laughs> but he was repatriated. At the end of the war, he went back to Germany and his first job, of all things, was working at an American Air Force Base. Then he went into various other businesses like shipping and furniture, and the like.

Q: We're going back to your research. What other types of pitfalls or roadblocks did you run into?

Jackson: Well, I guess when I first started, I was impressed with what I thought was the scarcity of materials. But actually, the materials were there. It was just a matter of digging and finding them. As I mentioned, I spent many an hour at the PRO doing nothing but turning pages in these huge, huge collections that they have, waiting to turn a page and see anything that had to do with the KMF-26 with particular reference to the Rohna. And the materials were there; you just had to find them. So that was one of the pitfalls and then I always tend to get in a hurry when I'm doing research or writing. I had to slow myself down and sort of take stock from time to time to see where I was and where I have been and where I wanted to go. So those were a few difficulties with the research. I had help. At Western Kentucky University, I had a couple of graduate assistants who helped me find material, and I had a couple of librarians who were very good at finding material. If you're a professor at a university doing research and writing books, you'd better have a good library. And we don't particularly have a good research library at

Western, but we do have a good scholarly resource library, and a bunch of dedicated librarians who will do just about anything to find material for you, so I had some help. And I acknowledged that help in the preface to the book.

Q: So was it the United States or England where you got most of your information in terms of your research?

Jackson: Probably the United States; because I heard from the survivors; John Canney wrote me a long, involved letter. And it's in the collection. I gave the collection to the University Archives at Western. Anybody could look at it if they want to. They just have to come to Bowling Green, Kentucky and go down to the archives and look at them. I got over a hundred letters from a hundred different survivors. I heard from their kinfolks and I heard from their friends and the like. Also there was the National Archives, as I mentioned, I went through; so most of the research was here in this country. But you see; it was a British ship full of American GIs, and an Indian crew. I had letters from Bombay, Australia (the Captain of the ship was T. J. Murphy from Australia). And so I heard from his daughter, I think just as the book was being published, I got a letter from her, telling me about his life and the like, so it was a very rewarding experience for me. And I am very pleased to have been a part of this story.

Q: And it was classified for fifty years?

Jackson: Well, you see, we talk today all the time about missile warfare. But, actually, this was missile warfare. I mean, this guy sat there and guided this thing down with a joystick. But we were actually the victims. We were the first victims of what might be called missile warfare, you see. And the British and the Americans definitely did not want their publics to know what kind of damage we had sustained. So they put a cloak of secrecy on it and the American records opened up well before the British. I think the British have stricter rules on opening up what was classified material than the Americans. They believed, and I think rightly so, that it would be damaging for the morale of the two countries. Personally, I could see that for the immediate aftermath of this event. I cannot, however, see all of the bureaucratic entanglements.

There were some GIs who had to prove that they were actually on the Rohna; that the Rohna actually existed. When they got to North Africa, one of the bureaucrats there said there is no such thing as the HMT Rohna, you see. That's what they had to put up with. In many instances, they lost all of their identification, they had to start from scratch and in all of that, mistakes were not particularly inevitable, but highly predictable. And on the other hand now, the Germans wanted full publicity. They wanted everybody to know. So their newspapers were full of the information about KMF-26, except that they were reporting that over half the convoy was destroyed and the like, instead of just one ship. They wanted people to believe that some thirteen or fourteen ships had been destroyed. Of course, that wasn't so, as we both know.

Q: Did they continue using those guided missiles?

Jackson: To some degree. We began to develop the same type of system and, interestingly enough, one of the founders of this system was Wernher von Braun, who became very famous in our own country. But, unfortunately, human beings are genius at making bigger and better war weapons, so these missiles began to be graduated from the Henschel 293 into systems that were much more sophisticated. I don't understand the technicalities, but we're always willing and ready and able to build a better war weapon.

Q: Since you wrote your first book, you've had it republished. Were there any new findings that may lead to a second book?

Jackson: In the second edition, I incorporated some of the letters that I've received from either survivors or next-of-kin or whatever, and at least one national newsman. Howard K. Smith wrote me a letter. In the Preface to the new edition, I didn't identify him, but I just said a "national newsman," but that was Howard K. Smith who wrote that. And when we set about bringing out a second edition … the first edition came from Naval Institute Press, so it was hard cover, and it stayed that way for about three, four years. The University of Oklahoma, which is a very fine University Press, expressed an interest in doing a paperback edition. So I got permission from Naval Institute and sent off the manuscript. But one of the editors over there said that he would not have a book from the University of Oklahoma with the word "tragedy" in it, which was the title of the book at Naval Institute. So he changed the title from "Forgotten Tragedy" to "Allied Secret." But the book is essentially the same.

Q: Anything that stands out more than anything?

Jackson: Well, there are a lot of human interest stories. In the research, I met a man from Auburn, Kentucky, which is close to where we live, and his name was Sam Cunigan. He had been on the Pioneer. And over the road about another fifteen miles was a man named Shelton who had been on the Rohna. Mr. Shelton and Mr. Cunigan knew each other. They had known each other for forty years. Neither knew that the other one had been on the Rohna and the other had been on the Pioneer, until I started work on this book. It came as a surprise to them.

I guess another very poignant moment was Mr. Richard Peach, who was a survivor in Pennsylvania. And he wrote and wanted to see what I had written. I guess I had written about fifty or sixty pages of the manuscript at that time, and ordinarily I don't send off incomplete manuscripts, but I said I'll do it, you know, I'll make an exception. And I sent it to him and I heard later that it arrived on a Monday, just after the Sunday night that he had died. He never saw it, but he wrote several letters to me in the course of this research and I incorporated much of his information into the book.

Q: Could you please give us an overview of the incident?

Jackson: Yes, the convoy KMF-26 started out in Scotland and it joined other ships at Gibraltar to go on into the Mediterranean, heading east, and the scuttlebutt was that this convoy was safe, passing through. One sergeant said that no ship had been sunk here in the past several weeks. Well, that was definitely not true. I list a whole page of ships that had been destroyed. And this convoy was sort of a sitting target. Air support had become rather limited because the previous year, the Allies had taken North Africa from the Germans and they had transferred much of the RAF and the American forces to Italy, getting ready for what would become known as D-Day later on. So air support was not particularly effective here. And it was about 4:30 in the afternoon when the German squadron, Geschwader, hit and they came from out of the sun, so that people firing back at them would have the sun in their face. And there were some dogfights; there was enough of the RAF left to engage many of the German planes. But the one that Major Dochtermann flew … he actually went on and flew over Oran, Algeria. One fellow, as he wrote to me, wanted to shoot at him, but he was ordered not to because apparently some other gunnery station had him in its sights, and they thought that was a better target, then he got away. Then he went way up and got up above the flack line, next he dived down and, to this day, there are many people who believe that his plane exploded, but it didn't, because he was coming down so fast that the carbon that had built up on his engines ignited and it looked like an explosion, but it wasn't. He finally got down, after he had flown the missile, he got down to within just a few feet of the waves that were cresting on the Mediterranean, and it was only very slowly that he was able to gain altitude, and then ultimately get back to Bordeaux in France. Many of the survivors from the Rohna were taken on over to what was at that time called Philippeville and stayed there for a time. Then they were put on another ship called the Takliwa and many of them were in mind of rebellion because it was exactly like the Rohna. But they made some changes. They made sure that lifeboats were in working order and that life drills, fire drills and the like would be conducted in an orderly manner. They made it safely to India and some of them to China.

That was the general overview of it and I'm sure there's more work to be done in reference to the Rohna. This is a very big story, as I've mentioned before, and it's something that deserves continued attention.

Q: Tell us about the Pioneer.

Jackson: Well, the Pioneer was a minesweeper and it was commanded by Leroy Rogers, who was called "Roy" for obvious reasons … "Roy Rogers". The Pioneer picked up the majority of survivors and we've all heard stories about how some of the Pioneer people jumped into the water, particularly one of them, Harold Jones who stayed in the water for several hours, in fact, plucking the survivors out of the Mediterranean. They put so many people aboard; I think six hundred or so; that its waterline was sinking pretty fast. And they got to Philippeville, I believe, about the crack of dawn the next day, rather early. They had to leave because they were becoming seriously overweight. They picked up a man named Don Zirkle and the Captain then gave the order to leave the area, and Mr. Zirkle quipped later that it was just like the Army to do things alphabetically. <laughs> So they got to Philippeville and stayed there for quite some time. There were the Clan Campbell and various other British ships that picked up survivors too, but it was mostly the Pioneer.

Q: I think we're all set. Is there anything you feel we missed?

Jackson: Well, I do of course feel very privileged to have been the author of this book and to have come into contact with so many great people. As I mentioned to my wife Pat the other day, it's sort of like family. So it's always a pleasure to meet survivors and their relatives and friends.

Q: We appreciate all the work and research that you've done.

Jackson: Well, it was my pleasure.

AN INTERVIEW WITH CHARLES LAFONTAINE

Rohna Survivor

Edited for readability

LaFontaine: My name is Charles LaFontaine from Champlain, New York. I volunteered for the services at Plattsburg, New York because I wanted to go in the Air Force. We were sent on a bus to Utica, New York for a physical and when we got out of Utica we wound up in Albany where they swore us in. We got a seven day furlough to get our affairs straightened out before we wound up in camp, you know. So I went back to Champlain and after the seven days I went back to Albany, we got onboard a train and they took us to New York City, then to Camp Dix, New Jersey. I thought that I was going to wind up in the Air Force when I found out I was unassigned. In other words, I didn't know where I was going.

I wound up in a barracks with all Chinese who hardly talked English. They were jabbering away in Chinese. Well, low and behold, that's why I wound up in China. You know there was a coincidence there. I said,

"Ain't this something?" I started off with Chinamen and I'm winding up with Chinamen, so I thought that was kind of curious.

Well anyway, we got on a train at Camp Dix and we headed out West. We wound up in Camp Atterbury, Indiana, not too far from Indianapolis, and that was a Company B 31st Signal Corps that I wound up in. So there we trained for a couple of months to be pole linemen, you know, stringing field wire, open wire and cable, and we went on maneuvers in Lebanon, Tennessee in the Spring of '43. When we arrived, there was snow on the ground which was unusual for Tennessee, and we had these pup tents they call them; it was a two man deal. One guy's got one half and the other guy's got the other half, except that we couldn't sleep. We had to stand up. There were some trucks there so we got in the back of the trucks and slept. Well, during the next day they brought straw and hay in and put it down in the bed of the trucks and it was cold. Well about four or five days like that and they finally got these six men tents and they set them up. Next, we were on maneuvers for a good couple of months. So, we made all the rounds. I had been to Nashville, and while I was in Murfreesboro we had strung some field wire and some open wire. I got up there and I clip in a handset and I get the operator and I called my mother. She said, "Where are you?" I said, "Murfreesboro, Tennessee. I'm up a pole," but the operator let us talk. It was good, you know. Well, after the maneuvers we wound up back in Camp Atterbury and we were there for a couple of months again.

Finally it was the first of June I got paid and I knew I was getting my furlough the first week of June so I telegrammed my mother to send me $50. This was on a Thursday; we were going to leave on a Friday. They were giving us a couple days grace for a ten day furlough. I take my wallet and I put it in my jacket, on a clothes hanger. I go take a shower, come back and my wallet was gone; $90. I almost had a heart attack. Well, I had to wire my mother again.

Ace Baldassari picked up a collection; got $40 for me. Well that's why I never forgot him. The next day he gave me the $40, I got a cablegram from my mother again. I left on a Friday and the train was packed so I had to stand up for a long ways. I was only home in Champlain about two days and I got a telegram. The outfit was moving and getting ready to go overseas so I was to report back for service. I says, "I ain't going back. I'm taking my ten days." So I took the ten days and I got back on the 10th day. They said, "Did you get this telegram?" I said, "I visited relatives. When I got the message it was right in the end and just trying to follow and catch up with me."

So we headed for Camp Patrick Henry, Virginia. We were there for quite a while waiting for a ship, and I don't know probably three, four weeks there was a swamp there. Oh, there was bugs like you wouldn't believe, you know? Well anyway, we get ready to board ship and there was a German "wolf pack" they called them, so we didn't sail. Somehow the Navy was chasing them around and getting them. Finally we sailed out on the Liberty ship *Alexander Hamilton*. The food was terrible on there. We had two meals a day; breakfast in the morning and late in the afternoon; goulash. They had these big kettles. They steamed them and when I say it was "gook" it was "gook". Well, it took us 31 days to cross the Atlantic to Oran in Algeria.

When we got to Oran we went to camp. Now, the food in Oran was good. We were on what they call double rations. It was all canned stuff but it was fair. They had to fatten us back up for the kill. So we were there a good month I would say, and finally we went back to Oran and boarded ship. That's where we got on the Rohna. Now Company A had gotten on the Rohna, which was the first ship. That was a mistake. When we got there they moved them to the Rajula, so they made out.

We set sail Thanksgiving Day that morning, early morning. The sea was very rough with high wind and probably 10, 15 foot waves or more. Well, during the day it wasn't too bad, but when it became late in the afternoon ... I think it got dark around 5:00, somewhere in there in the Fall and around 4:00, 4:30. Now in this convoy was these ships, they called them decoy ships. They had like an umbrella in the front and in the back it would fold up. We didn't know what it was and it was just that part where you can see the pilot house and stuff. Well, when the aircrafts are coming over them things went down; they folded down. Talk about some fire power. I want to tell you there was some fire power then that was these ack-ack guns, 30 millimeter or 20 and they had these cannons right up that were putting ack-ack in the air.

Q: So where were you during this?

LaFontaine: At the back end of the ship was the Chaplain's quarters. I got up on deck and we were on one of the main decks and we were playing deck shuffleboard. (Me and Red Berry, a big guy from Eerie, Pennsylvania). Anyway, we were standing there and a PA system on the board said, "Everybody below deck. We're under attack." We knew we were under attack. We could see the planes going around and the ack-ack. Bang. This missile hit, and we didn't know what it was at the time. I found out a couple days later they said it was a plane that hit us, because this thing looked like a plane. It had wings, it had a tail assembly on it, the motor was in the back. It was like a jet engine in the back. I did not see this. When I come to I was sitting against the guardrail and this guy, Red Berry, he must have blew right over the ship. Two guys picked me up because it took the wind out of me. So I stood up and it was a funny thing. I had just gotten these life preservers and nobody told us how to use them, so common sense tells you how to, and you could adjust them. There was a buckle you had to unbuckle and it tightened it up. Well, what happened when the guys were starting to get off the ship, there was two oxygen tubes in there. When they squeezed this, they didn't unloosen the belt to full expansion. Pow! Pow! Blew them up in the sea. I said, "Oh my God, those things are blowing up right and left," so I says to this guy, "Don't squeeze the thing. Take the tubes out and open it up, put it up under here," and it had two other tubes in the back where you could open a valve and blow in it, breathe in it, you know? So I put the two tubes in my pocket which helped to float. Well, a lot of guys lost their life preserver because of that. Nobody told us how to use them. Well anyway, we got in the water and it was just before it got dark.

Q: Had you gone back down?

LaFontaine: No, I wouldn't go below deck. There's no way. In fact, the back of the ship was all on fire. I don't know what was burning but it was a terrible fire on the ship. So, I went back as far as I could and I could see where the Chaplain's quarters was all blown to hell, you know? So the guys that were in there didn't have a chance, and there was a lot of my buddies in there at the time. Well, I come back up front because it was listing and dipping towards the back like the bow was coming up. The water was coming in the back side. I got up front and this guy was still up there telling everybody, "Below deck. Everybody below!" Everybody was going ape, you know? I said, "That guy's got to be nuts." Those that were below couldn't get up because they blew the staircases, and you know it had these hatch things over the cargo hold part and that all caved in and a lot of guys got it over that. When we got on board ship we were put way down to the bottom, and it was cold back there. My barracks bag, everything was down there. Well anyway, I said, "This ship's going down. We've got to get out of here." So I said, "I'm going to get off on the high side." The other guys that got off on the low side, some of them guys got burnt bad and probably never made it, because the fire was … This is hard to explain, but if you could see it, it was blowing out like … I think it was diesel fuel that was burning; because fuel will float on water and it was a bad fire. So, I went off by the bow, and it had a rope. You've seen these rope ladders? So I got off on that but it wasn't hitting the water. It was probably ten feet short, because the ship had listed, so I had to drop about ten feet and I was afraid that my life preserver would bust in, but it didn't.

So, I start swimming, which I could swim and well, it got dark and I wanted to get away from that ship. I was afraid it would blow up or the suction would get me. Now, it must have been a current, not only because I was swimming but I got away from there kind of fast, you know? Well I have to say then it was a long night because I looked at my watch and it stopped at 2:00. I can remember that, and a long time after then I see this light and I says, "I'm seeing things, hallucinating." Down you go, back up you go in the waves. There were a lot of waves. It was very bad. And then further distance I could see dawn. The dawn was coming, which I was glad to see, so that meant we were in that for about 12 hours.

So finally after a while I was starting to see a ship. So it pulled along and it had a spotlight; a big spotlight going, and they were picking up guys. When I got on there was quite a few guys on board, and they were all doing the same; rinsing their clothes off and throwing them on a pile and just standing with their pants on, and I did the same thing. Some guy helped me. Well, I finally lay down on the bunk beds and I fell asleep. When I woke up we were in the port of Bougie. I was the last one off that ship because I fell asleep. The guy who woke me up and got me out of there said, "You got to get out. We're in port," so when I come up on deck I got help to get up the stairs. I got off the ship and I'm facing the front of the ship, the bow, and that's where I saw it was a French ship they said translated in English it was "little fish".

Next I wound up in an ambulance and they carted us off to the hospital. It was the 69th British General; I found that out about 55 years later. This one guy used to come and visit me in the hospital, Gabe Hollis, and he's dead now, but I met him in Clark, New Jersey at a reunion. The guys were sitting at my table, and they said, "Do you recognize this guy coming?" and I looked and said, "Yeah, that's Gabe Hollis." I stood up and walked towards him and he was with his son. I says, "Gabe, where was I when you used to come see me in that hospital?" "Oh, Fontaine." He tells me 69th British General, and that's the first time I knew where I was in some 50 some years or close to 60 years, because I never saw anything going in and didn't see nothing going out, you know? That's where I got all the British clothing. That was one good thing. I had British shoes and they were better than the Americans; more comfortable.

Right after that we got reorganized; I thought we were going to invade France from the south, so I said I want to volunteer to be on the invasion to France because I could talk French. So they sent me to an MP station as an interpreter, which was a racket. I get assigned to a captain. I get a jeep, and my first assignment was to go outside of Philippeville. The French Army was stationed there, Charles de Gaulle and what they called the FFI at that time. So I go visit the head captain. So we get there in the jeep and I told the guy at the gate, I said, "We've got to visit your commanding officer to get the supply list," so he escorts up to this tent and walked in and there's this guy sitting down with three stars, and I recognized him because I had seen pictures of him; Charles de Gaulle. I had no insignias on me, so I start talking to him and asking him what they needed and he gives me a slip, so we got talking. Anyway, we had a drink of wine with them and it was good wine, and he asked me my name, where I was from, and he thought I was a British soldier at the time. I says, "No, I'm American." I told him part of the story about getting our ship going down.

Q: What was your first impression when you saw the Rohna?

LaFontaine: Well that was funny because Oran goes way down in the bottom and it's just high, it's on the bluff, you know, and it's steep. It's a hard time to walk, you're almost trying to run down there and you see these huge ships and we didn't know which one we were going on, so I thought it was a pretty good sized ship. Now some guys complained, they said the food was bad. I thought the food was good because we only had that one day of food. It was Thanksgiving Day so we had turkey, canned turkey. Now that to me was good. It's a good thing I ate because a lot of the guys got seasick. The ship was rocking quite a bit, even in port, but I ate. That was the last meal I had for quite a while, I tell you, because the afternoon dinner, or supper, we didn't make it. The ship was hit then and probably sunk by then. So I thought it was a pretty good ship.

Like I said, they had the chaplain's quarters in the back. And he probably got it too. It was a good size room. We could play checkers, ping pong or sit there and play cards and stuff. Well, they asked us not to stay too long to let some of the other guys onboard ship get in there and rotate like they call it. So I says to this guy, "We'll go out and play deck shuffleboard." You could do that on either side of the ship, right on the deck. So we got out there, we were playing shuffleboard and me and this Red Berry were on the end towards the stern. Now the other guys were up front. The deck is pretty long. It's a pretty good sized deck and there was other parts in it, but anyway when the raid started, looking over the side and like I said, all them ships, there was decoy ships that was a surprise on them because there was a lot of them. Then I saw the pioneer and there was a submarine in this convoy. It was surfaced at that time. Well, when the combat started they disappeared. They dove under, but these decoy ships, oh good heavens. It was deafening, the artillery shots, you know, and they call them ack-acks. Then of course the British had some ships in there that were called corvettes and they were smaller than the destroyer, but they were fast, and they fired. I personally saw six planes go down. Now I think at that time they were ME-109s. I didn't get that close to see them. Anyway, when we got hit the ship was on fire bad. I said, "Boy, I've got to get off of here." I was afraid when it went down I didn't want to be on it, so when I did get on it, well that's when I wound up in the water for so long. But you asked me my impression.

I thought it was a pretty good ship. I remember a lot of guys complaining that said it wasn't, that it was filthy and all this. I didn't see that. I thought it was pretty fair compared to going over on the Liberty ship; that was bad. My comparison was like, well if you put it in category one to ten and ten being the best, the Liberty ship was one. It was real bad. The HMS Rohna was a ten in my book.

Q: Did you lose some good friends?

LaFontaine: Oh yea. We lost 60 percent of our outfit, and the operating engineers lost a lot of troops. We got a lot of replacements. Oh God, we had all kinds of replacements. We stayed in Bizerte quite a while and I don't remember the name of that ship that we got on in Bizerte to India.

Anyway, we wound up in India and landed in Bombay. We stayed in port for a couple days, and they wouldn't let us off the ship for the first day but the second day they let us off, and I was amazed because there was leprosy. It was all over the place. Fingers all disfigured; they were beggars. They didn't have nothing, poor people. I didn't like Bombay. Well we stayed there like I said three, four days.

Finally, we got on board some trains and they were nice. There were cabins like, you know, the one cabin could sit about four people in and the beds come down and all. It took us a week to cross country from Bombay to Calcutta. And we got to Calcutta, we got on some trucks and they took us inland. They had a lot of air bases there. There were B29s that had landed there. We were putting communications into these bases. They were separated, because they were big bases at the time.

AN INTERVIEW WITH EDWIN W. LINVILLE

USS Pioneer, AM 105

Edited for readability

Linville: I was born here in Forsyth County, North Carolina in 1925 and attended high school here and went in to the Navy when I was 17, right out of high school.

Q: What made you join the service?

Linville: Well, everybody was going in and you felt pretty patriotic. All your friends were going and I was scared to death I wouldn't pass the physical so I really wanted to go, and the reason I joined when I was 17 was they were drafting you at 18 and they would put you where they wanted you, Army or Marines or so forth. You couldn't select when you were drafted, so I joined.

Q: How did you pick the Navy?

Linville: I've always liked ships and the water. I enjoyed every minute being on that ship. A lot of guys didn't like it. A lot of guys got seasick and so forth but I enjoyed most of the time anyhow. I was scared several times and the funny thing was when we first were attacked during the Rohna action I was not afraid or scared until afterwards when I got to thinking about it and heard about the two guys being wounded, and this thing could hurt you. It really hit me then.

Q: What happened after you joined?

Linville: The Navy sent me to a radio school in Noroton Heights, Connecticut, close to Stamford, and I attended radio school there for three months. Then I was transferred from radio school to the USS Pioneer, a fleet minesweeper, and went aboard in October of '43.

We picked up a convoy out of New York and went to Oran, Africa. We were there over Thanksgiving, November 25, 1943, and we picked a convoy up going to Bizerte, Africa. After leaving Oran on the 25th we were headed for Bizerte and we were under an air attack which was our first time in combat and it was all new to us. We were under air combat I guess for about two or three hours, something like that, at different times.

We thought the glider bombs that we saw were planes and we had a couple of them that were close to the ship went off, exploded, and I believe there was two men wounded from that. It seemed like the Germans were trying to get the escort ships at the tail end of the convoy so they could move in and get closer to the troop ships and that's what they had tried to do was shoot those glider bombs at us.

When they hit the Rohna I was on a 40-millimeter antiaircraft gun at that time so I could see very good but at first when we saw the ship it was leaning over pretty bad and smoking and on fire and we couldn't see any troops at first. Then we moved around to the port side of the Rohna and we saw all these soldiers in the water. To me, when I first saw them, it looked like pictures of seals in the water that I had seen as a kid.

And then the captain secured all of us from general quarters and we started picking up the men out of the water as best we could.

There were air attacks right after they had sunk the ship and they came in strafing our ship and they strafed some of the soldiers in the water. It was kind of hard to pick up the men. We put these cargo nets over the side and when the ship would roll over, the men would hold on to the rope. Then they'd get up so high and then we'd pull them aboard the ship. We did that for I don't know how many hours. We also picked up a lot of little Asian men and they were so tiny some of them they could sit in the sink in the head where it was warmer. We picked the survivors up until it got real dark, and even then the captain had the men in the pilothouse throw floodlights on the water so we could still pick them up after dark. And he did that until one time we had a contact for a submarine they thought and we had to get under way. Then we came back and picked up the rest of the men that we could.

One of the things I remember seeing is a soldier with a full pack on. We tried to pull him in but he slipped on the ladder and fell down and they swept a light on him and you could just see him going down, down, down in the water with his arms moving like that. That was one of the worst things I remember seeing and we could do nothing about it because the sea was so rough. Finally we pulled in to a small port there in Africa and took the men off. I believe we had six soldiers that had died during the night and they were on the back of the fantail of the ship. That's about all I can remember.

I remember seeing the pharmacist's mate; he was a second-class corpsman. I was in the mess hall one time helping a guy in and the pharmacist's mate was in there doing his best to save some of the men. He was the only medic we had really. He did a good job. He was transferred off the ship not long after that.

Q: One of the things that have always gotten me is you've got the Pioneer. It's a relatively small ship with a crew of 100 roughly and you pull in 600 guys. Where did you put them?

Linville: I don't know. That was one thing that I think the captain was concerned about but he made them go below. There was a lot; the engine room was full. They were right beside the toilets and the showers and stuff and we packed them in there. A friend of mine, Carl Schoenacker, he was one of the soldiers we picked up and he went up in to the radio shack. He said he was up in the radio room and there were four or five other guys packed in also there but they packed them down below as best they could. There was quite a few topside also, but I remember we had to go to general quarters several times.

Q: During the attack, when you were on the 40-millimeter, did you help pull men in?

Linville: What the captain did was secured everyone from general quarters and as those that were not on duty to run the ship were topside and helping pull the men aboard. After I come down off the gun, I come down on the main deck and didn't know exactly what to do to start pulling the men in. There was a gunner's mate on there who told us to cut this cargo net down and how to tie it on. He showed us how when the ship rolled we would pick the men and it'd come back and we would pull them in right quick. The captain picked the men up as long as he could see them or find them. It must have been after 12 o'clock when we left the area and headed for Africa; which was not far from where we were.

I understand since then that this area that we were in was a good area for the Germans to attack. It was close to France and they could pick up the convoys and have air attacks on a lot of them there. There were several ships sunk in that area after us, after we had left, and that was just the beginning because none of us had been in combat and after that's when the war really started for us. We were in the invasion of Anzio and later on the invasion of southern France and we never had any more casualties after that so we were very lucky.

Q: What were the conditions like in the water? I've heard different stories.

Linville: Well, it was very rough and it was cold and extremely windy. I've read different stories about that it wasn't that rough out there but it was because the ship was rolling very bad and the only way we could pick them up was to let the ship roll down and grab them and get them back on, but it was in November and it was cold. I don't know how those guys survived as long as they did.

Q: It was amazing. Some were out there so many hours. Did you know if your gun hit any of the planes or just kept them back?

Linville: We just kept the planes from coming in on that end of the convoy. We were shooting at them but I don't think we ever hit them. But we made a lot of noise and smoke up in the air and kept the bombers away from us. Other than that, they would have hit probably other troopships and maybe the escorts too.

Q: You said you saw a number of the men being pulled in. What was the worst that you saw of those men in the way of injuries?

Linville: Burns. A lot of the men were burned and the flesh was just hanging down from their face and arms and so forth. That was the worst I think and a lot of those little guys that were crewmen on the Rohna were from India ... their clothes were just burned off of them from the bomb. I'm sure there must have been a lot of them covered in oil. I know when I went in to the mess hall and saw these guys and they were burned real bad. They had oil on their clothing and arms and stuff.

Q: Where was the Pioneer relative to the Rohna when it was hit?

Linville: I'm going to say a half a mile or a mile from it; that's when I first saw the Rohna. We were really occupied looking up at the sky and trying to shoot at the planes and so forth more so than watching the ships and the convoy. I don't think we saw the ship until the captain said, "Secure from general quarters," and everybody left their guns and so forth where they were and started pulling men in.

Q: Were you there watching when the survivors got off the ship?

Linville: I was not. I was on watch. We had to continue our different watches after we got underway and I had the 4 to 8 watch in my radio shack and I didn't see them leave, none of them.

Q: Tell me a little bit about what happened with your crew and your ship after the Rohna.

Linville: Well, after that we did other convoy duties until they had the invasion of Anzio. We stayed between Anzio and Naples on convoy duty back and forth and sweeping mines also. The German planes would fly in at night and drop the mines and so we'd have to go out the next morning and do the sweeping and sweep channels in to Anzio and then we'd head for … with a convoy of empty ships to Naples, and that night we would bring the convoy full of material and stay there until the next morning and we did sweeping mines mainly. That was our job. And then there was the invasion of southern France and we had to sweep mines in to the beaches and open up channels so the landing ships could come in and bring the troops in. We were usually some of the first ships in for the first day or so opening up channels for the troopships and the LSTs to come in.

Here's another interesting fact ... Later on, they brought aboard our ship a radio and some officers and they would try to jam the glider bombs that the Germans used. They used them at Anzio and southern France. They had a radio room with transmitters in it and they tried to jam those glider bombs so they couldn't guide them and they would just go anywhere after that. I think they used that in the invasion of France. I'm not sure.

One last thing I want to say ... A few years ago, I wrote to the personnel in Missouri and asked them to send my records of everything from the day I went in the Navy. It listed the different places we invaded, what we did in convoy duty, and the invasions of France and Okinawa and all that, and it was a pretty thick stack of papers. And throughout the whole thing there was not one word mentioned about the Rohna. All these other places that we had been to and had actions that were mentioned in detail. Not one word about the Rohna, of the whole 2-1/2, 3 years I was in service. I thought it was kind of strange really.

LOUIS R. MARKIEWITZ

Rohna Survivor

Excerpts by permission from the *Antelope Valley Press*
Sunday Spotlight January 7, 2001
Written by Don Jergler

On November 26, 1943, in the Mediterranean Sea, the Rohna was part of a 23-ship convoy headed east for the Suez Canal. Ultimately, the convoy was to steam into India, where the men aboard the Rohna would join forces with China in the Burma-India theater.

It was a mellow afternoon on rolling seas. At 36, Markiewitz was much older than the other servicemen aboard the ship. While most had barely reached adulthood, Markiewitz had worked in the gold mines in Death Valley and at various construction jobs. Keeping a cool head, knowing when the odds are stacked too high—those are the things that life teaches best. Markiewitz had learned many lessons, and his experience would soon be put to the test.

At dusk, the attack came … Bombs dropped: gunfire rang out: a deafening explosion rocked the vessel and scattered the group of craps players into oblivion.

"It was an awful explosion," Markiewitz recalled. The lights went out and he found himself several decks below.

With the anguished and panicked screams of men and the war above enveloping him, Markiewtz made his way through the darkness during a three- or four-minute blind, stumbling trek topside.

He rappelled from a rope hanging off the starboard side, then let go when he reached its end. The cold water stung.

Hours went by and Markiewitz had found a 10-foot board he used to help keep his head above water and to conserve his strength. Fighting cold and rough seas, Markiewitz also battled the loss of sanity that forced solitude seems to bring.

Then he ran into Web, an acquaintance from his company who'd left from Pearl Harbor at the same time as Markiewitz. The two instantly recognized each other. Web grabbed hold of the board, and they both hung on. Little conversation passed between the two. But soon, Web began to tire, He complained that he couldn't handle it, and Markiewitz knew something was wrong. But he had no way of telling what the problem was, so he had no way of helping his companion.

Web's complaints stopped, and as quickly as he'd come, he let go of the board and swam into the night. "Web! Where are you going?" Markiewitz hollered. There was no answer. That was the last of Web. Markiewitz was alone again in the night.

As more time passed adrift, Markiewitz floated past a noisy group standing in one of the lifeboats. "Some of them were praying. Some of them were cursing," he said. Even from 50 feet away, with the water dimly lit by the moon and stars, Markiewitz could see their fate playing out. The men were thigh deep in water in a slowly sinking lifeboat. Markiewitz kept paddling past.

At midnight, Markiewitz began a grim assessment of his situation. His life was running out. "I gave myself two hours," he said. "I was so cold that my whole body trembled."

If he was going to die, at least it wouldn't be alone. "I heard some voices and one of them sounded like one I knew," Markiewitz said. It was a man named Ashworth, a friend he'd met before the war.

Four men were floating in a circle, and Markiewitz joined them. There was a man from his company, Cranston, who was having trouble treading water. Cranston asked Markiewitz for help. Markiewitz told him to keep moving, but Cranston said he couldn't. Markiewitz had an extra life preserver, which he put around Cranston's waist.

As soon as he did that, his attention was abruptly attracted by what appeared to be a spotlight flashing over the water. He peered into the dark, waiting for another flash of hope. In an instant, as he was waiting for a second flicker, one of the five men grabbed hold of him and took Markiewitz under.

Too weak to resurface with the weight of the other man, Markiewitz broke loose and made it to the surface just in time to see the lights from a destroyer staring at him. He quickly swam around to its side, and two British sailors threw him a rope. "It slipped right out of my hand and I didn't have the strength," he said.

After several attempts, they pulled him up a dozen feet to safety. "I got on deck and collapsed," Markiewitz said. The sailors put him in a hammock and exchanged his wet clothes for some dry ones. After getting warm and sipping tea, he had enough strength to walk about the deck to watch rescue efforts and look for his companions.

On the ground, he saw a body collapsed under a bench. It was one of the others with whom he shared the water. He'd been pulled out of the sea, but had succumbed shortly after that. He looked for the other three, but discovered that none of them had been brought aboard. He never heard from them again.

Update by Michel Walsh:

Sgt. Louis R. Markiewitz served in the Army Air Corps in Company C of the 853rd Engineer Aviation Battalion. He had three children and was married for 60 years. He lived to be 98 years and 5 months of age. His wife Nauwausau from Mojave, CA, sent me the news clip to include in this book.

AN INTERVIEW WITH ABE MARKS

Rohna Survivor

Edited for readability

Marks: My name is Abe Marks; I live in Wayne, New Jersey for oh my God, about 50 years now. Okay, well I was not born in Passaic, but I really grew up in Passaic. I was born in New York City, Harlem I guess it was. I went to school in Passaic through high school. About a year or so after high school, I went in the service, did basic training in Miami Beach, then radio school up in Sioux Falls, South Dakota and Madison, Wisconsin and from there we went to Tennessee and Jefferson Barracks and went overseas from, I guess it was Newport News, Virginia.

Q: What unit were you with?

Marks: I was basically a radio operator, voice, mostly code, where we spoke or communicated station-to-station, some ground-to-air, air-to-ground and it was done in code. I was in there for I guess 2.5 years before the war was over and came home. Got to the Liberty Ship we shipped out of Virginia and landed in Oran. We were there about maybe a week and a half and we transferred to the Rohna. I guess we went down on the 26th of November. We got on board the day before.

Q: Can you describe the ship?

Marks: Let's put it this way, it was really was indescribable. It was an old tub, even at that time the ship was maybe 22 or 23 years old and there wasn't much maintenance on the ship. It was old and it was dirty. What I did notice was the lifeboats that they had, I couldn't see how they would be able to even launch those things, which turned out to be true. They had just painted over all the davits and everything and they just couldn't be launched and they weren't. The Indian crew used axes to try to cut the things down and they did and they were the ones that took a beating. They died trying to get into the lifeboats. They had no sense of responsibility to their so-called passengers. The amount of so-called training, rehearsal of abandoning ship as far as I was concerned was nil. They passed out these belt types of life preservers that were inflated by using two cartridges, compression cartridges that were supposed to fill them up and they really didn't. But the backup was a tube which you blew into and the life belt expanded. And you had to keep it down at your waist. If you kept it up too high it wasn't good. You know we had no real instruction on the use of it. And the story that I think is interesting is the story of how I really survived this thing, pure luck.

For some reason I was assigned to guarding a prisoner. I couldn't understand where they keep a prisoner, why would they have someone in a brig? It wasn't for me to think about, but I did and I asked and they said just you got to guard this guy. I said where is this guy going to go? Where can he escape to? Well anyway, they took me all the way down to the bottom of the ship really below I would say ballast on the ship. That is how low they had this little jail. I would say it was not much more than 5 by 5 or 6 by 6, not much more, just room to have a bunk in there and maybe there was a chair. Well I went down there, I was taken down there. My prisoner's name was "Fitz". He was a red head and they called him Red, but whether it was Fitzpatrick, Fitzhugh or whatever it was.

That is the only thing I ever heard of the guy. He asked me to sit down and I sat down on the one chair and we played cards. He had a deck of cards. We played for a couple of minutes.

I said what in the world did you do? What the hell did you do to get down here? So he said, well I got drunk in Oran. I saw one of my officers. He didn't like me and I didn't like him and I beat the crap out of him. He was part of this engineering outfit that was building the airfields. And they took him; put him in the brig and that was supposedly the end of him you know until ... They weren't going to leave him behind because he did serve a purpose to them. What they were going to do when we got to India, who knows? So we are sitting there and talking and he says I got to get out of here. He says this place is foul, it stinks. He says, bring me up topside, I have to go on sick call. I said I can't do that. He just says, go ahead up. Tell them that your prisoner is sick. This guy might have been two or three years older than I and really experienced and he was telling me what to do, guiding me. He said go up and tell them that your prisoner is sick and then we will get going.

So I go all the way up, I don't know how many, three, four, five decks or whatever. And I go where they were holding sick call and I tell them, I say my prisoner is sick. He said, okay bring him right up. So I brought him up, bucked the line actually. He goes in and I waited for him at the rail. And looking out over the water there was a submarine that was part of our convoy. And all of a sudden you hear these sirens going off on our ship and there was a destroyer, I guess maybe it was the Pioneer, I really don't know. The submarine dived, disappeared, and then the air raid started. So we were told to go down below and get off the deck, which we did.

We tried to get to any portholes or whatever they had down there. The only thing they had was one of these cargo doors to open up and we really shouldn't have opened them you know for whatever reason, but everybody thought it was a real lark. I never saw the bomb come down. I never saw where it hit. But when it did hit, everything turned black, dark. It completely shut off the power. And it didn't take long you know, 'till some of the dust started to clear where I was able to see down there. The ship was listing a little bit. So I said hey, whoever was down there was going to get up topside, which we tried to do. But the stairwell was blown away. It was all rubble, but it was enough that we were able to climb on the rubble and almost reach the top and there were guys up there who could give us a hand and pull us up and get us on deck. And I met oh at least two of my so-called buddies. The group that I came over, we were replacement, radio operators. We were a group I think of about 110 men including officers.

Q: What was happening on the deck?

Marks: Well I was on the deck with a couple of my friends. By word of mouth because nothing was working, by word of mouth, we have to leave. The Indian crew, they were wild. They were just terrified, really terrified. They got these boats and tried to launch the boat and they really couldn't do it because everything was painted over. It was not in any operating condition. And they, however they jumped into the boat trying to get it down. They had an axe and they just cut one of the lines, and I saw the lifeboat hanging on one and these guys falling out of the boat. Either they were drowning or they hit on the side of the boat and they destroyed themselves. I saw a couple of life rafts going over. I said to myself, this is not for me. If anything, I am just going to get in the water and try to take off as best I can. It would be a horror, I saw what was happening on the life raft that was already out there and the fellows are on there and everybody was fighting for it. That kind of a fight I knew I wouldn't be doing very well.

In order to get into the water you would have to go down this cargo net, and I was standing there with a couple of guys. One guy I do remember very well was a fellow named Leo Rewkowski; he says to me, "you know I can't swim". We were all calm. It was amazing, this little group there we were calm. There was no hysteria that I had heard other than the native crew. And I said to Leo, I said don't worry about it. I said get in the water and just paddle away. You will be all right. Well I went into the water.

I never saw anybody. There was no one near me. I was able to hear things, but there was no one near me and I couldn't see because the swells would be up four, five feet and you are down low. Even when you went up you still couldn't see anything until I got about maybe 200 feet away from the ship and I turned around and I took a look and saw the size of the blow out on the one side. It was tremendous. It was maybe about 10 to 12 feet high and about 20 feet or 30 feet large, complete blow out. And that is all I was able to see in the water and I kept going until I saw the Pioneer.

I didn't know it was the Pioneer until later. I saw one of our boats and I got to it and I got to this one rung and I went up as far as I could. I couldn't go any further because I had my clothes on and the shoes were water soaked and I couldn't move any further. But there were a couple of sailors onboard and reached down and grabbed me and just flipped me over on the deck and so that was it.

The interesting part to this whole story is that if this guy didn't get drunk and land in the brig and I was assigned to him and he didn't ask to go on a sick call, I would have been stuck down there with this guy when the ship was hit and never would have been able to get out from down below. So whoever, through all the years you know I always thought about him and I never really did anything about him. And when we started these reunions in 1993, the first one being in Gatlinburg, you know I asked around to maybe I would run into him there. And as the years went by, I thought more and more about it and I checked with a lot of people that I thought were in that outfit and no one seemed to know about this Red. He said, yes I remember one, but that was about it. I finally got one guy, it was a semi positive thinking, information and I called up some guy up in Idaho or Iowa and I got him on the phone and I asked him if he was the Red that I knew. He said no, it wasn't me. And we talked for awhile and that was about the size of it, other than the fact that he was on the Rohna, but that was about it. And basically that is the story.

Q: Tell me a little bit about when they pulled you aboard the Pioneer. Where did you find yourself? Where did you stay until you got into Philippeville?

Marks: Where did I stay? Basically I stayed on deck. I went down below deck once and I was able to scrounge a cup of coffee. There were no dry clothes. There was nothing I could change into. I guess it was through the night you know, I and a couple other fellows were on the deck and there were obviously a lot of people in the water yet and we might have pulled a half dozen people out of the water. The ship went down and the deck was almost level with the water. And when it came down if there was anybody there, they had hands that we grabbed them, we pulled out. So we pulled out maybe a half dozen of the guys, and one of them that I remember pulling out is still here, a fellow by the name of Al Procton. He is here with his family, which is very nice. And that is about all I really remember about that, other than the story with Leo Rewkowski, who I met later. I never saw him onboard the ship. I met him later and I asked Leo, I said how did you make out, you know not being able to swim? He said it was just like you said. He said I got in the water. He said I moved so fast, he said the top of my shirt never got wet, so I was thankful for that.

Q: Did you see the ship sink?

Marks: That sticks in my mind through all the years. It had turned dark. I was in the water maybe an hour and by the time I had got onboard the Pioneer it had turned dark. I am not that, I can't verify the time, the various times, but it had turned dark and we looked out to where the Rohna was and it was in flames and you saw the thing tip up and went down. That was it. It was utter darkness. After it went dark, there were still a lot of people in the water. I saw a lot of them being strafed. You couldn't see the airplanes naturally, but you saw the red tracers going in the water after some of these guys. How many were killed that way, I really don't know.

Q: You said, when you were in the water you couldn't see anything but you could hear. What kind of things did you hear?

Marks: Oh, people moaning you know, yelling back and forth, but that is about it.

Q: Hear anybody singing?

Marks: If they were singing I wasn't paying attention. The ones that would know more about them singing would be those that were on the raft. And the stories that I had heard later about what was happening on these rafts, I am glad I never really went for one of those things. If somebody tried to get on the raft, they were actually beaten off. You know there was no more room. They'd get somebody on it, the whole thing would have tipped over and they would have gone, which a lot of them did too. They were hanging on to the sides and a lot of them went that way. I never saw it. I never saw personally rafts in the water. There were no lifeboats, because they were absolutely gone. There wasn't anything worthwhile about them.

In later years, I condemned the British for putting a ship out in that condition. And I am sure the United States would have to share in that too by allowing American soldiers to go on that ship in that poor condition. It was in very poor condition. As far as I am concerned, their culpability would be in the fact that they had no real plans instructing soldiers how to act, what to do in the case of an attack, how to abandon ship. We really had nothing other than being issued a life belt, which was fair as far as I was concerned. I understood this; you follow your own thinking. I never took my shoes off. If I am in the water, I said I am going to stand up, because I know if you are in the water, especially salt water you have a tendency to float. If you float, your feet would come up, your head would go down. So I figured that I would wear shoes and it will keep me in the vertical position. One of the things that they did say, make sure if you have to jump off the ship, don't wear a helmet, which was good advice. If you went with a helmet, water would come in there and it would break your neck, so I got rid of the helmet.

The next morning we were taken into Philippeville and the British Red Cross was very good to us. They issued packages and had pants, a shirt, a heavy sweater, socks, underwear and shoes. We wore those for the time until we were re-outfitted by the United States Army. The reason we stayed in North Africa for the time that we did was that they had to interview us. All our records, the records went with us on the ship, so we had to go through the whole series of shots. We were there maybe five to six weeks before we shipped out again.

Q: Were you injured at all?

Marks: The truth of the matter is no. The cargo net went down just so far and then I dropped into the water and I banged my back. And I had a pilonidal cyst, which I was not aware of. That made me aware, because after that I had this lump on my back and that was the end of it. I went on sick call and the doctor looked at it and said yes you have a cyst there. He said it's opened up now and he gave me some band aids and whatever and that was the end of that. I never thought it was worthy of a purple heart or anything and I never made any application for it.

I guess you are aware of the fact, you know that we were told not to write home about the Rohna sinking, not to say anything about it, that it would give information to the enemy. If the enemy didn't know what they were doing, shame on them.

I guess we are not kids anymore. I was 83 last week and maybe I was one of the younger guys. The average age I would say of our group now would be about 84, maybe 85. So there are not too many of us left.

Q: When you were helping pull guys aboard the Pioneer, what kind of shape were the men that you were pulling out of the water?

Marks: Well they were still in pretty fair shape. They were able to help themselves, you know it was difficult. You had nothing other than somebody giving you a hand. That is what we would do. The length of time that I was helping I really couldn't attest to. It might have been a half or three quarters of an hour. Then we had to stop doing it because the Pioneer had to pull out and they were worried about being vulnerable themselves. At that time they must have had about 600 people on and Captain Rogers and his officers were concerned that there was enough to possibly capsize their ship. So that was that. They did a tremendous job. They saved 60 or 70 percent of the survivors.

Q: Can you tell me about the difference between the young guy that went off to war and the young guy that came back? How did the experience affect you?

Marks: Well, you know I think about something like that once in awhile, comparing it to the young guys today and going back in the last maybe 20 to 25 years. You know the complaints about Vietnam and things like that, we didn't understand. We figured we fought the good war. There was never any thought about going up to Canada or any place. We enlisted. A lot of guys did not enlist. I enlisted. You know maybe I was a little bit altruistic at the time. I wanted to enlist December 8th and my mother would not sign for me. So by August or September I got my notice. And once I got my notice I said okay now I am going to enlist and I was able to talk my mother into signing for me. I enlisted in November of 1942; went overseas after so-called training and when thinking about it I guess the training really was minimal, physical training was very little.

We left Miami Beach in January. Yes we were restricted New Year's Eve and we left there the first or the second of January. It took us approximately two days from Miami Beach to Sioux Falls, South Dakota. That was a shock going from a temperature in the 80s. When we got off the train, in Sioux Falls, South Dakota it was 18 degrees below zero and the temperature averaged in January and February, close to 38 degrees below zero, so that was a little bit on the cold side.

Q: I would say. When was the first time you actually told somebody about the Rohna that wasn't involved with it?

Marks: Here is an interesting side line to that. You know I had one sister. She was older than I and her husband was drafted before I went into service. He went overseas. He ended up in North Africa in Oran like I did and he shipped out from Oran to Italy, Naples on the Rohna, a month before I did. From Naples he came back to Oran and that is where we got on the ship. So I told him, and that is when he told me, he said yes I was on the ship the month before. So through the years, my sister and my brother-in-law went down to live in Florida and he was the one who saw an article in the one of the papers down there talking about somebody had written looking if there were survivors of the Rohna. So he knew the Rohna and he knew that I was on it. So they called me and told me that there was interest in the survivors of the sinking of the Rohna and the name that was there was John Canney, Ruth Canney's husband. So from there you know I had some communication with them. So they had my name and address and they were the ones, they were really one of the prime instigators of getting us together and having the first reunion in 1993 which was the 50th anniversary of the sinking of the Rohna. So through them I was with a fair amount of people that went to this reunion in Gatlinburg, Tennessee.

Q: Has anything in the modern time keyed you off, like a gentleman has mentioned watching the Titanic when the ship goes town, brought back a memory?

Marks: For whatever reason that didn't impress me. What used to impress me was where you would see a war movie and seeing ships hit and then go down. That always stuck in my mind, seeing the Rohna flipping up and going down. That picture sticks in my memory.

TOM MERKER'S PERSONAL ACCOUNT
Rohna Survivor

While sailing on the Mediterranean Sea at about 4 p.m. we were attacked by a German aircraft and hit by a bomb. All hell broke out. Everyone was running in different directions. The crew was basically Indian. Part of the ship was on fire. A friend, in my outfit who was a very good swimmer told me to stay with him. The rope ladder was lowered and the life rafts were also lowered.

Many of the soldiers were jumping off the ship. My friend and I climbed down the ladder and noticed that the soldiers in the water looked like a swarm of bees. As we climbed down the ladder we observed that the life rafts were falling down and hitting the soldier's bodies and killing them from the weight of the rafts. My friend went down on the rope ladder and I followed him. When we finally reached the water, he took me to a life raft that was near us. There were about 6 of us hanging on to the ropes on the life raft and we tried heading towards the ship that was waiting to pick up survivors. When we got to the ship, the others started to climb up the ladder. As I put my left hand on the rope ladder, an Indian crew member who was part of the six on the life raft stood up on the raft and jumped, grabbing the rope. His feet pushed the raft away and I couldn't hold on to the rope ladder. The waves pushed me away and now I was floating on the raft alone. As I was floating away, I could hear the soldiers screaming that were hit the by the flying life rafts. In addition, the ship had a very big hole from the bomb and was burning. You could hear the men screaming of those caught in the fire. I floated away by myself. It was getting dark and I picked up stragglers, as the waves took me away from the ship.

As we were floating away, we decided that the best thing to do is if one man on each comer of the raft would hang on with his body from the waist up on the raft and feet in the water, we could balance the raft that way. It was really very hard to do it for a long time. The waves were too high and too strong. The waves would turn the raft over. If you didn't let go in time, you would end up under the raft and drown. You had to be lucky to be close by, so that you could grab the rope and hang on after the raft turned over. As time went on, we lost several of the men that way. We said that no one was to be on top of the raft. One of the men stood up on the raft and kneeled and looked up and prayed to god that he was a married man with children, and not to let him die. In no time a wave came and knocked him over and he was gone. That single incident caused me a great deal of pain all my life I constantly have nightmares over that incident.

The next thing I remember was waking up in a British hospital. I asked the British doctor what happened. He said that a British patrol boat was sent out in the early morning to see if they could pick up any survivors. They saw me hanging on to a raft and I was unconscious, but still breathing. They immediately brought me to the British hospital. I was in the cold water for 16 hours. They kept feeding me hot tea with rum to warm me up. I was there for three days and then they transferred me to an American hospital. I was there for a week. I couldn't eat or drink much because everything tasted so salty from drinking all the sea water.

After my stay at the American hospital I was taken to a camp where all the survivors were. They were reorganizing, so that they could continue on to India. When I arrived at the camp I was told that was our destination. The men in my outfit couldn't believe what they saw. My officer briefed me and told me that I was not to speak of the sinking of the Rohna not even amongst ourselves. He advised us that anyone caught talking about it would be court martialed.

We arrived in Bombay, India on February 1, 1944. I was stationed at an airport in Bangalore. The bomb that hit the ship was a radio controlled bomb. Before I was to be shipped home and discharged, I was awarded the Purple Heart.

After I was discharged I got married to my sweetheart. In April of 1946 I went to the V.A. in NYC to try to get some help for my constant heartburn. I steadily had heartburn from drinking and swallowing salt water. During my time in the service I lived on Tums and Rolaids. My heartburn continued after my discharge from the service.

I told the person interviewing me about my experience and I needed help for my heartburn. He put me on hold and said he would be back shortly. When he did come back he said that he was sorry, but there was no such incident on record. He said there was nothing he could do for me. For approximately 55 years or so the incident was kept a secret. I got nowhere.

In 1982 my wife and I moved to Florida where I tried to get help, but to no avail. In 1998 I went to the V.A. in Rivera Beach, Florida and was finally acknowledged. I have lived with nightmares about the incident. I was finally given a disability for P.T.S.D. in the year 2000. In 2004 I was given additional disability for my back as well.

My father received a telegram saying that I was missing in action, but never received one saying that I was found.

Needless to say how disappointed I am with the treatment I got from the government and the V.A.

AN INTERVIEW WITH DANIEL MIDDLETON
Rohna Survivor

Edited for readability

Middleton: My name is Daniel Middleton. I was born in Dallas, Texas, in 1916. I was pulling 1-A classification and I didn't want to be drafted and have them just shove me anywhere that they wanted to so I enlisted in the Air Force, thinking that I might be a mechanic, that's what I enlisted for. I kept coming out different orders, different things like cook and finally it came out communications so I said, well; I might as well take communications so that's where I ended up. It was the AACS; Army Airways Communications. And we took care of all communications in the different airfields,  the radio range, point CW, which is international Morse code, and anything to do with communications and I was an operator.

Q: Now, when you joined, what was your family's situation?

Middleton: Well, when I joined, my wife was pregnant with my daughter and it's one of those things. I hated to go but I would have been worse if I had waited and was drafted. So I felt that was the best thing to do.

I got some of my basic training in Fort Devens and then I went to New Orleans, more training there. Next was Smyrna, Tennessee and then on to Jefferson barracks, which was an embarkation camp before going over. And, from there, I went to Hampton Roads, Virginia, and I left from there. It was a funny thing. The fellas kept saying did you see the liberty ship? I said, "No, why?" The name on there was Henry Middleton. So we went over on the Henry Middleton across the Atlantic to Oran in North Africa.

Q: What was that trip like?

Middleton: Well, that trip was a little rough. During the war, they made a lot of these liberty ships, which were, I guess, thrown together. I had to sleep in a hammock and there were rows of hammocks and they'd squeak all night long. I had a sleeping bag so I slept out on deck most of the time. I couldn't stand it, being cooped up in a hold on a ship. So we went across with no incidents and went through the Mediterranean to Oran, passed the Straits of Gibraltar, saw the Rock of Gibraltar and the slopes of Morocco on the right-hand side. And we arrived in Oran and we were safe there.

Q: What was Oran like?

Middleton: I never got into town. We weren't there very long. I would say we were only there about a week and we stayed in camp. We got in a little trouble while we were there. There was bad rainstorm came up and the ground was like clay and it gets awfully slippery and, when anybody had to go to the latrine, they had a little problem, if you know what I mean. Other than that, it was pretty quiet there.

Q: So tell me about getting the orders to go aboard the Rohna and what your first impressions were of the ship.

Middleton: Well, one morning, they said, "Fellas, we're leaving." That's all. They marched us down to the ship and we went on board. We went up a ramp on the side and onto the ship. Well, I looked at the ship and I don't know: we got to go on that? So it was an old ship and they used it to go from England to India and it was all Indian crew. And when this accident happened, they all jumped overboard, most of them.

Q: Where was your group stationed on the ship?

Middleton: We were on the second deck there was one below us. It was more to the back of the ship. There wasn't anything there but a bunch of bunks and there was a space in the middle, they had a table, we could play cards, that's about all there was there. Well, we saw tarantulas there, which were about an inch high and running around the ship. It was actually an old tub, I would say. The British weren't noted for the cleanliness of the fleet, I know that.

Q: What were you doing when the ship was attacked?

Middleton: I was out on deck playing shuffleboard and, all of a sudden, these planes were coming down, swooping down over the ships and, in the distance, and I could see one aircraft had been hit. It was spiraling down just like you see on television or in the movies and I don't know if it was one of ours or one of theirs. And then, about that time, they ordered us to go below and we went below and started playing cards and just sat there until we heard this loud explosion. The hatch covers went flying up in the air and the place filled up with smoke. We couldn't get up the stairs; they were all blocked with debris so we had to go up through the hatch covers to get up on deck. When we were on deck, I was up there just a short time and I could see that the ship was starting to burn and I thought, I got to get away from here, fast. So I climbed down a cargo net into the water and just swam as fast as I could. A lot of them stayed onboard because they were there at gunpoint. They were told, "You stay here. You don't get off." That's after I'd already gone.

Q: When you were on deck before they sent you down below and you were watching what was going on, was the Rohna or the rest of the convoy reacting with gunfire or anything like that? What was that like?

Middleton: They were trying to knock down any ships that was around but this one here got through and released this little glider bomb. It was a radio controlled, and it was in an experimental stage and the first time that, I guess, they had used it. And it really worked for them. That's one of the reasons, probably, they kept it a secret. They didn't want the Germans to know how efficient it was.

Q: I'm backing up a little bit. So you go up the ladder to the deck after the ship was hit and its smoking and burning, what was happening, on the deck?

Middleton: Well, one thing, like I say, they made the fellas stay on. They didn't let them get off the ship. That's when the Pioneer came in. It pulled up alongside and took most of the ones that were there. And, well, I went into the water and I swam fast as I could. I looked back and I could see tracer bullets shooting out of the ship and I kind of turned away. I looked back again and the whole thing was ablaze and then it just disappeared into the water.

Q: How much time do you think went on between you getting in the water and …

Middleton: There's no way of knowing that. Everything is done on instincts. You don't realize what you're doing, really. You're not yourself when something like that happens, you know? Instinct tells you to do certain things and you just go by that.

Q: What were you wearing when you got in the water?

Middleton: There's a belt that you put around your waist which has two chambers and, at the beginning, there's tubes of carbon dioxide. You push that and it blows the tubes up so it keeps you afloat. You grab it and put it around your waist.

Q: Tell me about your time in the water.

Middleton: Well, the sun was just going down when it happened and I was picked up in the morning just as the sun was coming up.

Q: So you were in a long time.

Middleton: All night long, yeah.

Q: Tell me about the seas and anything you saw or heard.

Middleton: The sea was kind of rough. We weren't bothered with sharks because the water was quite cold in November. There were porpoises around … But it was just a battle all night just to stay up. The air went out of my belt, a couple of times. I kept blowing it up and it kept going down so I saw a couple of dead bodies floating around and I took the belts off them. They didn't need them anymore. I put one under my legs and one under my waist and the one that I had in the middle. I floated around there and you'd see ships, you wouldn't know how far away they were at night. You'd see the lights and you'd yell and they didn't hear you. Toward morning, I could just see the sun starting to come up and I let out a yell and they put a spotlight right on me.

Q: While you were in the water, did you hook up with any another men?

Middleton: Yeah, when I jumped over, I swam a ways and there were a few of them there and we all got together in a group and they kept going off, I guess, drowning during the night. And, toward morning, I was all alone.

Q: Did you see bodies or other survivors at that point when the sun started to come up?

Middleton: No, not at that point.

Q: You were kind of all alone?

Middleton: Well, it was dark and I just wouldn't know whether they were around or not.

Q: Tell me about the actual rescue when they came and found you.

Middleton: Well, they put this spotlight on me and, previous to that, I said one prayer. All night, you're trying to survive and you don't think about things like that. I guess it was just a very short time after that I was picked up.

Q: How did they pull you out of the water?

Middleton: A fellow dove in and pulled me out. In fact, I corresponded with him after the war and he told me that this ship that had picked me up was sunk the next day.

They asked me if I wanted a cup of cocoa or a drink of rum. I says, "Well, I think I'll have cup of hot cocoa." They brought it to me and I think I took about one sip out of it and I was gone. I ended up in the hospital. I woke up in the hospital in Bougie, North Africa. It was pretty much like any hospital only all the beds were in one room. They didn't have separate rooms. They were all in one room.

Q: In the hospital, did you see anybody you knew?

Middleton: No, not really. Like your friend Chuck Finch, and all the others that got on board the Pioneer and there were a lot of them out in the water. If it hadn't have been for that rescue, there would have been a lot more drowned. But the Pioneer did a good job. The ship was so full that they couldn't squeeze in any more. Well, there were other ships, evidently, that had picked some up but I know the Pioneer picked up the majority of them that survived.

Q: Where did your unit regroup after you got out of the hospital?

Middleton: Well, there were several ports along the coast. There had been bodies, dead bodies floating in and survivors came in and all of these survivors were shipped to Bizerte and we all got together there in Bizerte to continue our trip on to India. It was amazing. You would think certain ones would survive this and they didn't show up and ones that you would least expect survive were there. Mainly the ones that survived were on the Pioneer.

Q: Had you made any friends before the incident that you were looking for?

Middleton: No, not particularly. We were kind of split up after we took our basic training. Went to different camps and some went on to mechanics school, some went on to radio operating school, which I did. There were a lot of different units on there, a lot of them from out west, signal corps and engineering groups and all kinds of different units.

Q: Do you have any fond memories of your friend Chuck Finch?

Middleton: Oh, yes. Chuck was a good friend. He and I worked in the radio station there in New Delhi, where all the planes came into New Delhi and he and I worked together for two years there at the radio station and we became good friends. He was a little different than I was. He was one of these fellas that liked to have a good time and go out and enjoy himself, have drinks and so on. I just stayed around and thought about home and family and read. When the war with Japan was over, everybody was celebrating, drinking and I drank a little too much and Chuck took over for me and he did a good job. If it hadn't been for Chuck, I don't know what would have happened.

Q: Now, after the war ... tell me about your homecoming.

Middleton: Well, it was November the 25th, I believe, in 1945. We were shipped into Camp Kilmer, New Jersey, and, while we were there, we went into the mess hall and on the table were quarts of milk, plenty of butter, all that sort of stuff, which we hadn't had for a good long time so that was a happy homecoming. We came into Long Island Sound with whistles blowing and ships going by and when I saw the Statue of Liberty, I got a lump in my throat so glad to be back.

Q: What do you attribute your survival to?

Middleton: Well, I think that I had been around salt water so much and knew how to work with the waves and so on and so forth. I knew that, if you swallowed any of the salt water, your throat would swell up and, after awhile, you wouldn't be able to breathe. I think that maybe faith had a lot to do with it. In fact, I know it did.

I'm glad to be alive. I'm 89 years old and so that's the way it was intended to be. I was able to retire and move to Florida, I was there 26 years and I started having a little problem with my arteries clogging up. I was in the hospital three times so I figured the best thing to do was move back and be near our children and grandchildren up here in Rhode Island. My wife died of a brain tumor in 1999. So I'm lucky to be alive.

AN INTERVIEW WITH IRVIN MILLER

Rohna Survivor

Edited for readability

Miller: I volunteered for the Air Force and was inducted in Fort Sam Houston, San Antonio, then went on to Wichita Falls to Sheppard Air Force Base and got two weeks of basic training. Next I went to Sioux Falls, South Dakota for radio operating mechanics school which was a 13-week course. I couldn't get interested in the mechanics end of it, so they sent me to Madison, Wisconsin for the operator's course there. Then went to Smyrna, Tennessee for overseas training and from there to Jefferson Barracks, Missouri for some more overseas training, and finally to Newport News and was shipped out of there on a Liberty ship, I don't know the name of it, and went to Oran, North Africa. We were there about 20 days, and then got on the Rohna.

Q: What was your first impression of the Rohna?

Miller: It was actually a junky looking ship I thought. To me it was an old ship and hadn't been taken care of too well. And then in the evening we heard shooting going, and of course some of them were looking out of the portholes and saw planes. Then the guns on the ship started firing and

I thought we were hit then. But when we did get hit, all the hatch covers flew off and the ladder going out of our hold fell and was on the third deck. People on the second deck had to help us, lift us up through the hole where the hatch covers had been, and then they had a ladder going from there on up to the top deck. That's how we got up on top side.

They ordered us overboard the moment we got up. When I got up there I started for the low side because I figured it wouldn't be so far to the water. There was a major on there, he says, "Soldier if I was you I'd go this other side." I went there and crawled down a cargo net and of course it's still a long ways to the water. Then I just dropped off into the water. And it didn't take long for the current to wash us away from the ship, whereas on the other side, the current coming against the ship was washing some of the men into the hole where it was burning.

I floated off a ways, and there was about a two-foot wide raft that came by and two other guys and I caught it. And we floated out a ways and one of the other ships was coming through. One of the men suggested turning part of our raft loose and swimming in order to catch this ship coming through, hoping that they would drop a line. But by the time that ship got where we should be catching it we'd already floated way on past, swimming hard as we could trying to stay back. But then I floated on; we separated there. It was dark by that time and I floated looking, listening, finally I heard voices, and so I swam for them. It was a full raft, and it had two people on it that were hurt and a row of men around it, another row around them, and I made a third row. And the second row was holding on to the back of the first, the third row holding on to the back of the second one, and you just had to hold your head up because the raft was under water. And we floated I don't remember how long, a pretty good while.

Then we saw lights out front of us and we floated right into the side the boat. They threw down about a half inch rope line and it landed on my shoulder and I caught a hold of it. I saw where the raft was going to turn over and we couldn't all get up on that little rope. So I turned the rope loose and went for the raft and floated on again for a pretty good while. And this thing, it was a tugboat, called the Mindful, came out front of us again. So I turned the raft loose and swam for the boat. And they threw down about a one-inch line, and I was too excited to tie on like I should have. But I just got a hold of it and tried holding it while they'd pull it up. And I was just about to clear the water somebody latched on to my legs and we both went down. But I came up again, at the rope, and I kept trying to catch it, get them to pull me up, but I didn't have the strength. I asked them if they didn't have a ladder they could lower, and they did. So I run my leg through one of the rungs, and at that time the tug listed the other way. Well I fell backwards but my leg was holding on. So then when they listed back the other way well the water washed my back up and I rung my arm through it and they pulled the ladder up. And that's how I got up on the Mindful.

Q: Irvin, let's go back a little bit when you first got up on the deck. Can you tell us some of the activity that was going on at that point?

Miller: Well the crew was busy but they got me off the ladder and told me to go to the side, and I just more or less splattered on the deck and I crawled away from where they were working. One of them told me I should go down in the hold, that it'd be warm in there. My teeth were chattering and he told one of the guys to take me there. And so the guy said, "Follow me," and I couldn't walk. I started crawling. And he came back and helped me get up. I sat down on the steps and he would move my legs and then I'd get my behind down to the next step, and I went that way to the bottom. Someone that was already down there put me up in a bed and gave me some tea and I went to sleep. And then after sleeping awhile I was all right then. But when they finally quit picking; well we were pretty well loaded. They weren't finding any more survivors. We went on then to Bougie in North Africa.

And I was in the hospital a couple of days, and then the ones from Philippeville Bougie and Bone got on, we called them 40 and 8 trains, and reassembled in Bizerte. And then we were in Bizerte about a month and got on another ship and went on to Bombay, India. And there we were divided into where we were supposed to go, and I went to Bangalore, India, which was about halfway between Bombay and Ceylon, which is now Sri Lanka, and was in Bangalore about 14½ months, and then went on to Luliang, China, and was there 7½ months, and then flew back across the hump to Calcutta. And waited there a month and got on a ship and came back to the States. And landed in New York and they took us by ferry across to New Jersey to Camp Kilmer. And there they separated us again to go to the nearest place to where we lived to get our discharge. And I was discharged on the 11th of January in '46. And that's about it.

Q: Can we go back just a minute to when you were on the Rohna before you'd gone into the water. Can you describe some of the activity or what was going on up on the Rohna? You'd said that went to one side and then came back, but can you describe what was going on?

Miller: Nothing. I was the only one … this major and me. I didn't see anyone coming up or there wasn't anyone standing around. Everybody that had got up there had gone off. And so as I was coming out of the hold they were going overboard. Because I looked back afterwards, and of course it was dark then, I'd say it was dark; well you could still see the ship. And it was less than half of it still out and it was going under. And I was told it took about 30 minutes, for it to sink.

Q: Do you have any idea how long you were in the water?

Miller: I think it was about 4½ hours.

Q: Did these events change your life?

Miller: I try not to think of it, because the Rohna ... (upset, long pause) When I think of it this would happen ... (choked up; long silence)

ARCHIE AND ELWYN NELSON
Rohna Casualties

By Walter Holden

Something about the program on the History Channel stirred old memories. When I was three years old the family living next door suffered a terrible tragedy. Two sons of a widowed mother were reported to be "missing in North Africa." Later they were declared killed in action. I remember that there was always a sad mystery about their deaths. No one had any information about how they died. There was only a rumor that they were aboard a ship that was sunk in the Mediterranean.

I went to my computer and looked up History Channel.com; but there was no information about the ship. It was a dead end. Some time later the program came on again. This time I had paper and a ball point handy. I wrote down the name of the ship.

"Rohna" brought up a lot of web pages. I opened the "Rohna Survivors Memorial Association." The next step was to ask the local library to find me a copy of James G. Bennett's "The Rohna Disaster." I found the names of the Nelson boys in appendix "C" under "Casualty Roster". The sad mystery was solved.

Now I want all those people who might be interested to meet the Nelson boys and know that they had lived.

The picture is of Archie (L) and Elwyn (R) with me in the middle.

These pictures were taken in the summer of 1943. The last time the Nelson Boys were home. They were probably taken by my father. Since then they have been in Holden family albums. Over the years I have looked at them and remembered the good times that the Nelson boys brought to the neighborhood and how they had made me feel like I was one of their little brothers.

AN INTERVIEW WITH JAMES D. REIDY
Rohna Survivor

Edited for readability

Reidy: I was drafted when we lived on Long Island, New York. They sent us out to Old Camp Upton from World War I days. It was still in existence and still active, of course with the war coming it became more active. We took the test and what have you and I went to Miami Beach, Florida. The Army Air Corps took over a lot of the hotels down there. In fact when we had mess in a hotel restaurant. We were in a building about five or six stories tall. Next we shipped out from there to Scotts Field, Illinois, an Air Corps facility. I took a radio course, a high speed code operator; Morse code. You get up to speeds of 25 messages an hour you know. And from there we boarded a train and were ready to go overseas and we embarked from Newport News, Virginia. It took us almost a month to get across the Atlantic. The convoy was big and there were submarine threats from the Germans. As far as I know they didn't lose any ships. We proceeded on and docked at Oran, the western part of Algeria; close to Morocco. We stayed in Oran I would say for another month to a month and a half and that is when we boarded the Rohna.

Q: What was your impression of the Rohna?

Reidy: Well it was an old freighter passenger boat. Reading some of the literature now, I think it was built in 1926. So let's see, got on the ship and you know the dates, the day after Thanksgiving. They sent I think 30-35 aircraft, 30, but not all of them carried this new device which was a 1,100 pound bomb. It had stubby wings and I can identify it, because I saw it coming right at us.

Q: Where were you on the ship?

Reidy: We were with the AACS group, Army Airways Communications Service and we were attached to the transport command, Army transport or Air Force transport, which came down from home, Mediterranean, through the Suez Canal area, where all the news is about now, into Calcutta. That is where I eventually landed.

Q: Please describe the attack.

Reidy: We were one deck below the promenade deck. And we had tables down there that I guess ten or 12 of us sat and ate our meals. And there were two, three, four people designated each day on KP duty to take these pots and pans and go to the kitchen where they prepare the food, which was lousy, let me tell you. It was terrible, not enough and whatever we had was just, there were reports that the cooks who were English, were charging large prices for a sandwich, $5, $6, $7. The Americans, they are known for having lots of money, so that is why they probably charged us but it was a real bad deal.

But anyway, I had KP duty down in the kitchen. Outside the kitchen at deck level they installed these refrigerator boxes, walk-in things, which they had the meat and perishable products that needed refrigeration.

Well they were on either side of that level and they were right up against the side wall of the ship with a space of this much. When we heard ... we thought it was a drill until somebody said something and we went behind these boxes because they had shutters that lifted up. So we got there, we first went to opening up cans of pears. So we got out mess kits and we scooped up cans of pears and started eating, something we never had before. So we were behind this thing between the wall of the ship and we were looking out and right behind us was another ship that we could see. Something came down right in front of them, looked like an airplane. And I said, somebody yelled out and said hey we are under attack. Did you see that? And those of us that were looking out we saw it, came right down and exploded right in front of the ship. They missed it by about 100 yards, but enough I tell you it was tremendous.

I might inject that I can't understand, we were in sight of the Mediterranean coast of Algeria and I am sure there were Air Force planes around, why they didn't send them out? There was some sort of a dog fight, but it was nothing. So we watched this one aircraft in the distance and there was like a flash and this flash was coming at us and we watched it and it came down and went down past us. If it had hit mid ship, I wouldn't be here today and that is what happened and we were on our own for what we were going to do.

So a fellow at one end of that space came on out and he tripped over something. They had wooden finishes on the deck, teak wood that they used a lot of and that was stacked up like a cord of wood, but it was black and he couldn't see anything. And one of the gentlemen said, oh we can't get out here, it's all blocked. Well at that point outside the ship they had started letting down lines to try to get the lifeboats operating. Well a line came down right in front of us, and I went out one of those openings and so did a couple of other guys and went up. We only had to go up maybe five or six feet to the railing of the promenade deck.

I saw a fellow, last name was Donovan, one of our group and we walked around the ship to the other side. Now the ship was listing and somewhere in our training we were told if you ever got sunk and the ship listed, not to go off the low side, go off the other side. They had cargo nets let down to do this.

The bomb hit in a troop deck of about, it was 800 in that area. I think 400 or 500 got killed just like that with the explosion and it went through that area and out the other side below the water line. On the promenade deck was the hole with the flames coming out like a blow torch. So we left there. There was nobody that said abandon ship or what have you. In the meantime, we looked over the side. We went back to where we were before and looked over the side and the ship was opened up like you had a can opener and you just opened it up like this for a length of I would say about 50 or 60 feet.

Well, we had an Indian crew. There were crew members coming out, jumping on this piece of the side that stuck out like a diving board into the water. Nobody said anything about abandoning ship. People took it upon themselves to get off. So I got off with the fellow that was with me, Donovan, and he was joking you know. He was like doing the back stroke and making a big joke out of this thing, but it was really serious. He didn't realize at that time how serious it was, when news came in about just what happened that night. The ship went down about an hour and a half to two hours and it lit the area that at one point the planes came back.

I am talking survival now. I am up to what happened to me. Let me tell you that. We got off, lots of men in the water, swam away from the ship to get away so you don't get pulled down if it does go under suddenly. And we went and looked up and there was the Pioneer, the American mine-sweeper. It came up, it wasn't moving, we came up to the rear of it where they had these brackets that extended out from the ship. Whatever mines they picked up they put there to dispose of I guess whatever operation that was, I don't know. Well the seas were rough. And minesweepers came down and these were reachable, these brackets like a knee brace. So they get on, grabbed that, then the minesweeper would go up and they lose their grip and go down and the minesweeper then came down. It was just chaos, I am telling you. So I made a decision as I said to my son, the best decision I ever made in my life. I said I am not going to fight this. It is not going to happen. So I decided to go around to the other side, went by this group and came to the minesweeper from the other side, the seaward side at this point, not the landward side and I swam.

I just want to say that preparation for this trip overseas, we were in good physical shape. Wherever we went, after radio school they had us for a while in St. Louis. I forget the name of the army post. But boy did we, we got into a lot of obstacle course work you know. We were in good shape and I was very happy about that because it helped me. I just swam, and I tell you there wasn't hardly anybody there. They had the freeboard on the minesweeper. It is only about eight to ten feet. You go down that and you are right on the water, but they put these cargo nets down and that is what I swam for.

I was telling my son that I grabbed that net and I just held on and I just stayed there. All of a sudden I felt somebody grab me by the seat of my pants and they tied something around me, pulled me up and threw me on the deck. So I just laid there awhile, got my breath and composure, got up and said, gee maybe I can help these fellows you know. I went over to give them my help, pulled whoever came you know. They said no, we will do it. We know what to do. So they sounded okay to me. But we had 600, over 600, 605, I think to be exact on the Pioneer, and I tell you they were great individuals.

What they do, is that the minesweeper would move to a group of survivors that maybe were on some of the rafts that, I forget the terms for those and they had fellows in them, hanging on to them and there would be a group. If there was one person and there was a group, they would go for the group and if they got the one person fine, but they would go for the group. So they were doing that for quite awhile and then we suddenly got underway. They said the planes had come back or were still in the vicinity. So that is what happened and then they took us next morning to Philippeville; a port on the Algerian coast.

Q: How long do you think you were in the water?

Reidy: I would say maybe a half hour at the most, went in, swam away from the ship. The minesweeper was there, stopped, wasn't moving. That is what they were doing.

Q: Were you ever told or ordered not to talk about the sinking of the Rohna?

Reidy: No, nobody told me that. I just saw a piece of that article and I wrote home about it I am sure, but whether it was censored or not, it could have been. My wife was getting censored mail. I guess everybody had that experience. But that is about it. Not a long story but it changed me a bit.

Q: Did you lose some close friends on that day?

Reidy: Oh yes, a lot of people. But it was a big part of my life and when you are in the water like that, I never got the feeling that I wouldn't be picked up, you know out of all these ships somebody would pick us up. But for certain reasons, like how the mechanisms didn't work with the lifeboats for some of these rafts that they had. That would have reduced the casualties by quite a bit if they had worked properly. I think that Captain Murphy should have been … it was an English boat and he was an Australian Captain, but he was responsible. I mean what you do, you got a ship you should go around and see what it looks like to other people.

AN INTERVIEW WITH CARL SCHOENACKER
Rohna Survivor

Edited for readability

Schoenacker: I was in the 322nd Fighter Control Squadron at the time the Rohna was sunk.

When I graduated from college in June of 1940, the war was going on in Europe. I was a pacifist. My prize-winning speech in a high school speaking contest was, "War is a Racket" and it was taken from a booklet written by retired General Smedley Butler who I've since learned was also in China. He was in China in 1926, but he became a strong pacifist. And I'll give you the first line of that speech. "War is a racket. It is the oldest, the most profitable and the most vicious. It's the only one in which the profits are registered in dollars and the losses in lives."

I didn't know quite what to do. I was ripe for the draft, but I didn't want to be in those damn trenches of World War I with the mice, and the lice, and the mud. And I wasn't sure I could aim a gun at a man. So, on St. Patrick's Day of 1941, I enlisted in the Army Air Corps. I was not one who enlisted to kill Krauts. Now, men of my son's age went to Canada to avoid going to war. Men of my age who wanted to kill Krauts went to Canada to enlist, or men who had a very close European or a British connection.

When you go in the Army, when you enlist, you expect three things. You expect to be fed, you expect to be housed, and you expect to be uniformed. Of those three, the first week I had only one. I was fed. I went a week before I got a uniform. I froze to death in my civilian reversible coat and I was marching in Long Island. A temperature of 40 degrees and 30 percent relative humidly is cold. And so I was cold for that week. We were housed in a part of huge double hangers.

Pay was very low. First three months, I think, first three or four months, $16 a month. After that it went to $30, and that was what a good hired man on a farm got where I lived. So they didn't want many people in, but as they drafted more and more people, why then things changed.

And then in July I was put into an outfit that they were going to send to Iceland. Well in June the America First people found out we had Marines in Iceland and they screamed and hollered "Get our boys out of the war zone." Yeah, and they planned to do exactly that. They were going to get the Marines out, send a battalion of Army and a squad of fighter planes, but we didn't have fighter planes then. We had pursuit planes. Did you ever stop and think of where the P came from in the P40, the P38 and so forth? That's pursuit. We didn't want to fight in the period between those two wars. Armistice Day, the 11th day of the 11th month didn't celebrate soldiers; it celebrated the Armistice, the end of war. And it celebrated, it honored the dead and the Gold Star Mothers and the Gold Star Widows. It didn't honor the heroes who helped win that war.

I had a girlfriend I'd met in college and I was very afraid when I was in Iceland, she was a farm girl and she was a school teacher in a farming community and I realized that the farm boys were there and I was concerned that I'd get a letter saying she met one, but I never did. And so, we established contact right away and on July 7th we were married. Lippert had found a small trailer cabin, overnight cabins between Hartford and Springfield. And there was one open so we went out there and Ruth and I lived there and we had a wonderful life. We had a big lawn. Ruth found blueberries along the Connecticut River going to waste; we had blueberries every meal in season. She loved picking those and she knew how good they were for us. She knew nutrition. Pete would stop and see her once in a while. And Pete liked our life so well that he and Eva were married and we helped persuade them I'm sure, in fact she admitted it. So we had a good life there.

But Labor Day everything changed. I knew I was going overseas, Ruth had a good job, she was a Home Economics teacher. And Home Economics Teachers worked ten months. They were in demand and their pay scale was much better than others. And she got a job in an oil-rich town of Bolivar, New York. You could smell the oil. She didn't want to give that up. So Labor Day she left me, I went back living in the barracks.

Somewhere along the line we lived in tents there, but I can't remember when. So we went overseas on the libert ship Nicholas Gilman, I don't know when now, it was in October, we went to Oran. One of my disappointments was I always wanted to see the Rock of Gibraltar. I had heard so much about it. And it was foggy and misty and I never really did see it. There's an interesting family connection here. My grandfather, Joseph Schoenacker was Alsatian. And in the Franco Prussian War, 1870, when that war ended he was in Oran. We didn't have any Army history in our outfit, but my grandfather and I both had an Oran connection.

We were there, it was very cold at night, life there for me was kind of well … we were just waiting. And then of course we got on the Rohna on Thanksgiving morning and I still think the First Sergeant Ekiss was responsible, I have no proof of this, but we had very good quarters. The Rohna was essentially a cargo ship but forward there were staterooms. I don't know how many staterooms there were. And there was a big stairway down one deck to those staterooms. And that's where we were; where those staterooms had been. We did not have to go down any ladders. Now other people down below us, to get down into the holds where they were they had to use ladders, we didn't. We had the big wide stairway. If we heard the news, I don't think I had any news at the time, but the news got to us. If we got any radio news we were told that the troops overseas were getting turkey dinner and all this stuff. Some of the men were critical of our Thanksgiving dinner. We were moving out of the harbor when I ate mine and I thought, considering it was a British ship, considering the British had been fighting for what, five years? They were hitting the bottom of the barrel. And believe me the Rohna was the bottom of the barrel, but taking it all in consideration I thought that that canned chicken that I got, my biscuits were done properly; some said theirs weren't. I thought it was a good Thanksgiving dinner; taking in consideration all the facts.

There was a terrible roll. I've since been told that those ships had dampers to dampen the roll but they were inoperable. And the roll of that ship made many of us seasick. I didn't lose that dinner but many did. That I remember.

We bunked where we ate, we were in hammocks, and our hammocks were put away. Now other people were in their hammocks when we were hit. Our hammocks were all put away somewhere and we had footlockers and I can't for the life of me tell you who brought my footlocker. I didn't have to lug that footlocker aboard ship, but I don't know who or why.

We had the Thanksgiving meal, and the breakfast the next morning was what other people said it was alive, it wasn't good. People complained, but I was more understanding. I think probably because I'd lived with British in Iceland, I understood their situation. So I was more understanding than the average GI. And I was older than the average GI, and I was trained by regular army, so I was in the better shape really for an attack than others.

But I remember some time or other leaning up against the big rafts that were on a 90-degree. You just pull the pin or cut the rope and they slide into the water. I thought I could lean up against them, you know, but I couldn't. But in doing that I looked, well, it's a good thing we're not going to need these things, because they aren't going to work, because they were painted solidly. And the other guys emphasized all the rust they saw. There was rust, yes, but those things had been painted solidly to the platform they were on. Just like painting a window shut. And I knew that may have helped save my life, that knowledge. Did I report it? I don't remember, but one of our lieutenants was up there when I went topside, was up there trying to break it loose. That I remember.

I remember general quarters. I don't remember any lifeboat drills. We were supposed to stay in our bunking area. I went there, I stayed there. I formed a bond with a Sergeant Reid. He was a very religious person. He obeyed orders. He was much more proper than I was. But the amazing thing to me that was when push come to shove and we were attacked, he didn't stay in his bunking area, I did. And where he went, I don't know, but he is on the wall of the missing.

And I had understanding of the people who wanted to know afterwards, because I wanted to know about him. And one of the heartbreaking things of this whole thing was I'd signed his will. So his wife came to my sister's, which was the address I had, was my sister's address. And I couldn't tell her anything. When I came home, it was after the war then, I couldn't help her. She couldn't understand why I didn't know. But I didn't know what happened to him. I don't know what happened to him. I'd been told by one of the people who've researched this that he probably was killed in the blast, but I don't know that. But I stayed there. I was playing solitaire on my foot locker. I don't know what I was sitting on.

And when the ship was hit, I just remember a "thud." The cards went in every direction, and I've said this many times before. It wasn't wind, because wind has direction. And this had no direction. Cards went everywhere. They didn't go all this way, they went everywhere. I knew we were in trouble, but I didn't know how much trouble. The next thing I remember we were at the foot of the stairs, and seeing Ekiss at the top of the stairs, and he was calm. Said it was time to come up. I went to my foot locker, I picked the things I wanted. I left my .45, which I had at that time. I left my helmet, I wasn't going to need that. I picked up the one thing from my mother that I had. I had a pocket watch. And I brought that. And I wished I'd had a condom, I never thought of this. People save things in those. I had what I hoped was a waterproof money belt, but it wasn't. I can't remember what else I took, but I traveled light, that was my thought, travel light.

I went to the top of the stairs and what I saw was chaos. Pure and utter chaos! I've said this before, it hasn't changed. When I saw the hole I don't know. I saw something in the water, a lot of something. Those were heads bobbing along. But I went right to those rafts. One of our lieutenants was up there. I made eye contact with him, but I couldn't hear him, and I don't think he heard me. But I expected he wanted me to come up, and probably he had some tools where he was working. He just waved me to go over the side. I saw only one lifeboat. It was hanging on at a 45-degree angle, and men were walking right by it. So I didn't bother to go back there, there was no point in it.

Moment of truth. We had these lifebelts, CO2 cartridges, will they work? I squeezed it, "pssst," it worked. Whew! Because I couldn't swim. I could dog paddle. Went down the side, dropped into the water, and tried to drop on the top of a wave and be carried away but I didn't make it. I was trapped there. There was one man in our outfit that I knew that I saw in the water, and we made eye contact. He was a Polish boy, and he had no relatives in the United States. He was a good lad. He died in China someway or other. But he reported me dead, 'cause he knew I couldn't get out of that mess I was in. I saw him on his back swimming away. I thought, "Oh, boy, you're lucky. You'll make it," but I didn't think of not making it at that point. I mean, that didn't occur to me.

I floated by the hole in the side of the Rohna, and this was very early, because there wasn't fire coming out of that hole. There was some smoke coming out. But I got off the ship very, very quickly. Behind the ship I got caught in an undertow, and then I knew I was dying, because I was being pulled towards the bottom of the Mediterranean very, very rapidly. How I got loose, I don't know, because I sped out, fought it, or whether it moved away some way … I don't know. But anyway, I went down, I'm guessing, 15 feet. Then I came back up very rapidly, and kind of shot out of the water a little bit, went down a little bit then, and that was it. And then I was free of the Rohna.

There were two boys from the Appalachians; they were scared out of their hide. They saw my stripes. I never finished telling you earlier, I said that I was in the army a year before I got any advancement at all. In the next six months I went from buck private to staff sergeant. I was a private in March; I was a staff sergeant in October. And I held there for a long time. And I certainly expect to advance in the 322nd 'cause I didn't fit. So they saw my stripes, they were all over me. And if I did anything heroic, it was to calm them down, but that wasn't very heroic, because I had to get them off me before they drowned me.

An officer came along, and then we had to decide what we're going to do. There was what I referred to as a mass of humanity that looked like an overturned lifeboat as I looked off to my left that was quite nearby. We could get there easily. But off in the distance was this ship, and that had stayed there. Now if I can get to that, I'm home free. I looked at that mass of humanity, I thought, they can't help me, and they don't need me. So they went that way, and I went the other way.

So I didn't go very many waves before there were three or four men clinging to a jettisoned wing tank from an airplane. And it was the shape of a wing, it wasn't damaged, because it floated. And that was a lucky break, because there weren't a lot of those in the Mediterranean, and that was very convenient. There was one guy in charge, and he said, "Wait." And he waited for me to come on, and one guy yelled at him, "Ah, let's go!" But fortunately the guy in charge says, "We need all the men we can here." So they waited on me, and I got over there as fast as I could. And then we would get on top of a wave, kick like sin, and push ourselves down, and then kind of rest, and kick ourselves down. And we got to the Pioneer very, very quickly.

I have said that they went from general quarters to lifesaving without missing a beat. That is not true. They were doing both at the same time! They didn't go from one to the other. I've since gotten to know the Pioneer boys, some of them. I know Edmund Will said that soon as he finished firing, he threw the cargo nets down the side. When I got there, there were no cargo nets, they hadn't been thrown down, and they were still firing. There were six men with three ropes on the side I was on. And they'd drop a rope, you'd grab it, and they'd pull you up. I was last on, so I was the last off. And I was on the trailing edge of that wing, and then the guy on the leading edge let go of it. Oh, yes! It struck me right on top of my head. Oh, god! That hurt! I saw stars! I was a little bit dazed, that rope was dropped, and I kind of reached and it wasn't there.

And I reached for it, well, I was sworn at, "If you don't want to grab it, get out of the way so somebody else can!" Well, that woke me up. Next time it came by, I grabbed it, and boy did I go up fast! Before I even got to the deck there was an arm came under, it came under here and under here, and I was sliding across that deck.

Those guys were busting their butts to save lives! They could have dogged it; they didn't! They were working fast! I have great respect for them! Well, as I went sliding across, there was a bolt hit me here, my head hurt, and I thought, "Well, maybe I better go on sick call. Got nothing else to do here." So I inquired as to where to go, they told me exactly where to go, down one deck and back into a mess hall. And there was a bulkhead there, and I looked in that mess hall. Over here sitting were guys who're bleeding. And I now realize they were men from the Pioneer that had got hit by shrapnel. And the floor was, oh, about ankle deep in water, and covered with blood. I looked in there, and that was an instant cure. "I'm going to go in there and say, "My butt hurts, my head aches." No way! I went right back up topside.

I tried to talk to a guy. He said, "Just find a place." They didn't want to talk. They just wanted to work. They were working. They were great. I saw the Rohna sink. I've talked to a man whose job was sinking ships, and he agreed, that it's just an awesome, awful sight, even if you're doing it deliberately, it was an awesome sight. All of this color, which is really pretty. Fireworks. Really beautiful. And then it slides in the water, and suddenly there's nothing, and you are just as empty as the sea you're looking at. It just empties you.

I found a little four-foot square platform near the radio room under the bridge. And you go up three or four steps. And you had this platform and 90-degrees, and a couple more steps into the radio room, so that when you opened the radio room door, it was practically impossible for light to shine out on the sea. It was all hidden inside. That platform was warm. There were heat pipes, water pipes right there. I spent my time there, I slept there. I was alone. I took out my stuff. It was 8:00 when I got around. Opened my watch and it was running! It was actually running. But as soon as I let the salt water out of it, it quit. I still have that watch. I still have those works, but I got new works in it. We don't use those anymore, but I do have that watch. That was pretty much my Rohna story.

Q: Tell me a little bit about when you got to Philippeville.

Schoenacker: Okay. I don't remember a lot about getting to Philippeville, though. Now there's been some controversy about the sea. I didn't mention high sea to you. And I finally got it figured out, and I think this is correct. The people who said there were five-foot waves were correct. The people who said there were 12-foot waves were correct, because the sea rose during the night. When I got there, the waves were big enough so you couldn't see over them. One of the reasons I know that the seas came up, Edmund Will said that later on they were using the roll of the ship to help pull men aboard. As it rolled down, they would grab their arms. As it came up, as it rolled up, they'd pull them out. There was none of that when I came aboard.

I had taken off my shoes in the water. That lieutenant suggested it. I didn't leave them on the ship, I should've. That lieutenant I met, he suggested we take our shoes off. And we were barefoot, we were wet. We went to a British camp. We were across the road from the Mediterranean, I remember that. We were in big tents, many men in a tent. Not just a four or eight man tent. We had C-rations. C-rations came in hash, pork and beans, or stew. There was one of them I didn't like, and I think it was the hash.

Well, I had good luck, so the night before we left, why I didn't get in chow line early, I just wouldn't take the hash. So I wasn't going to stand in line forever, and I was in the tent all alone, and a Brit came in, stuck his head in the door, and he went through the flap, "Can I help you?" "I'm looking for the Sergeant." "What Sergeant?" "Well, the Sergeant." There were many Sergeants in this place. "Which Sergeant do you want?" "The Sergeant that wants the beer." "I'm the Sergeant! And I want beer!" So for a dollar I bought three, I assume they were liter bottles, they were bigger bottles of British beer. And I had some camaraderie then. I had no idea who the men were that I buddied up with, but somebody in the 322nd. We drank two of them. We went over and sat on the seashore, and we drank two of them. Well, I didn't much care for it. Then we found some drunken Americans, we traded the third one for a bottle of whiskey, of good high-quality whiskey.

So that next day when I got on the forty-and-eight; why I could sleep that first day. But that forty-and-eight ride was very depressing to me. Those boxcars which were marked on the side for 40 men or eight horses; which meant that if 40 men are in there they were treated like horses! And you had straw, you had blankets. That's about all, and it was depressing to me. And I remember one night, I remember some stops, it was just depressing.

Q: Let's go back onboard the Rohna. You go on deck, can you describe what was going on?

Schoenacker: I can't really describe the scene that was going on. My eye was zeroed in on what I should do. I was trained. I had expected to see Ekiss, I didn't see Ekiss. I looked out and finally figured out those were heads in the water. I knew we were in big trouble. One of the things that bothered me that I haven't mentioned mystified me because I was dumb. I saw this huge hole and the plates were blown out. Well, anything enters, it bends the plates in! I didn't have brains to realize that it entered, and then blew the plates out. And I knew enough to go over on that side, the side that it entered. I think it went in on port side. It was already listing the other way, so I knew that it'd gone right through the ship. But I went to the rafts as I told you. I didn't see anybody I knew. I saw people scurrying here and there.

Well, my son says I saw lots of guns sliding ... I don't remember this now. My youngest son was impressed that I said I saw a lot of .45s sliding around. Other than that, it was chaos, it's all it was. People were scurrying here and there. There was no organization whatsoever. It was every man for himself. Now I lived because I was trained to follow instructions and I followed them. But the men in the 853rd who lived, were not in the bunking area, they didn't follow instructions. It worked both ways.

I was dumbfounded. I really didn't expect we were going to ever be attacked. I had read that the Mediterranean was free of submarines, which was not true. That was just American propaganda. We all do it. Germans did it more than we did, but we all do it. And when I saw the Rohna sink, I had two thoughts that were both foolish, I guess. "I'm afraid somebody's going die." I should have known there were dead men on the ship when I left, but I was in a state of shock, clearly. The other one was, "I'll read about this in the paper." And the reason I didn't is ... one of the main reasons, we talk about our victories. Well, I knew the Germans would crow over their victory, but they didn't, because they released 20 to 30 of those things, and a victory would have been to get several ships, and they only got one. So they didn't crow, so they didn't think it was a victory. We didn't think it was a victory either.

Q: Later, some of the men have talked about a roll call where they were trying to establish who had survived and who hadn't. Were you at that roll call?

Schoenacker: If there was one, I don't remember it. I think probably there was. I remember when other ships came in hunting for Reid; that was the big thing. I was hunting for Reid. I was concerned. Losing him upset me; we were bridge partners. "Well, we'll play some more after we get on ship again." My partner was dead, and one of the partners against us was dead. This Vinny Orlando that I met went with the equipment and they saw a ship sunk in the Pacific and he was just bubbling to tell us, "Oh, boy!" when he got to Bombay. Boy, he got the shock of his life. Must be an awful feeling. It's one thing to live through it, another thing to suddenly have it hit you in the face like that. "Where's Reid?

One of the men who died on that ship, was a Tech Sergeant Jones. He was a loner but I got to know him. I'm not afraid to meet anybody, and he needed somebody to talk to. He was very wealthy, he loved his daddy. Chase Manhattan bank had all of his securities. He didn't need GI insurance, but just so we could have 100 percent he signed. He had insurance in Chase Manhattan bank and got $10,000 when he died. He was a very frugal man. Every summer he went to Atlantic City and he wanted a room, very simple room, take out the big heavy furniture. He was happy to sleep on the floor. He was a very interesting individual. He died on the Rohna. And the Polish boy that I met didn't die on the Rohna, but he had nobody in America, and his grandparents in Poland were his beneficiaries. Those two that I knew of, I thought of those beneficiaries.

Q: Anything I forgot to ask about?

Schoenacker: All right, you just reminded me. The weekend of the Rohna, my wife Ruth and a bunch of teachers went to New York to spend Thanksgiving weekend in New York City. The night that the Rohna was hit spoiled Ruth's evening. She knew I was in trouble. I never believed in that crap until it happened to my own wife! She knew I was in trouble! She was unhappy because I was in trouble. She didn't know I'd been sunk. She didn't know anything. She just had this gut feeling that something was wrong in my life, and it sure as blazes was!

How did the Rohna affect me as an individual? Well, I was depressed afterwards, but once I got out of the 322nd, when we got to China, the Army has one smart thing they do. If you have a misfit, you transfer them to somebody else. All right, they put me on detached service to the Chinese-American Composite Wing, CACW. There they were using that same equipment that I knew. I was in Army heaven. I could function. And I did function. I got on very well, and there I made tech sergeant, the last thing before I came out as a tech sergeant at the end of the war. But as far as affecting me afterwards … my wife said that my father wanted me to talk about it, and I wouldn't talk about it. Well, I didn't think he'd understand. In our first home where we lived, I didn't want to talk about being sunk. I tried to get information; but couldn't get any. So I just gave up. John Fievet didn't give up.

Q: When was the first time you were able to tell somebody about this story and they listened?

Schoenacker: Vinnie Orlando called me. He heard one of Charles Osgood's two announcements. I called Osgood in New York. They gave me Fievet's phone number. Yes, that was the first time; Vinnie and I had talked about it. But then from then on, I was obsessed. And one of the things that made me happy in my life is finding other people who were involved, who want to know. Pat Bonacci is here at the reunion in Nashville. Pat Bonacci read one of the articles in the Geneva Times, he called me, "Do you think my brother was on that ship?" "Well, what was he in?" "He was in the 853rd." Then I thought, "Does he want to know?"

His brother was probably body parts. He did. So he's been coming to the reunions.

Other people have written to me. One of the nice things that happened; I got some coverage in the Rochester paper when we dedicated the memorial in Alabama. A lady called who lived in a Rochester suburb, obviously British, first phone call that came in, she had been a nurse, I guess in Philippeville. She was so glad to know why they got all those poor suffering men that night. She always wondered for 50 years what happened.

And another big thing, I had a hand in helping John Lane get a memorial in Arlington for First Sergeant Ekiss, his father. He deserved it. Ruth and I went to Arlington when it was dedicated. We were the only non-family members there. And things of this nature, of bringing, spreading the word.

And when I come to these meetings, you see me talking to the people who were first-timers. Like Jim Bennett went to meeting after meeting before he found out anything about his brother. In Dayton, Ohio, a lady walked in the door, she saw some people, they knew about her brother. Before she even checked in she found out! But once you get involved in this, it can grow on you. So that's' how it's changed my life.

AN INTERVIEW WITH FRANK SCHULZ
Rohna Survivor

Edited for readability

Schulz: I'm a Depression baby; in the Depression it was hard to get a job. My dad was in the police department and he got me a job at what was formerly Spencer Lens in Buffalo, later on became American Optical. I got a job there and we were making binoculars and things like that. I didn't know anything. I didn't know a blueprint from a white print but I learned. I'm a fast learner. So we were there and the war started. Prior to that I had been in school and was studying for the priesthood for a number of years, until I found out about girls and then I left. When the draft started I had a couple of deferments, working in industry. Eventually I was drafted in July of '42. I was born in 1919 so I was 23.

Q: Tell me about what happened before you went overseas.

Schulz: I was inducted into the service at Fort Niagara and through testing I was sent down to Miami Beach, Florida. The Air Force had taken over many of the hotels in Miami Beach and I went through basic training down there. And I think we were tested down there for some area as to where we were going to go and I was sent up from sunny Miami

Beach, to Sioux Falls, South Dakota, to the cold. I went to radio school there, communications, and learned dits and dots and dashes and all about taking radios apart and putting them together. I didn't know AC from DC at the time and I was selected to go to Officer Candidate School up in Sioux Falls, South Dakota, was interviewed and so forth. I did well in the school and I went from there to OCS in Valley Forge. Next I went to Yale University; the Air Force had taken over most of Yale and I was commissioned there.

While I was at Yale, right before that I had met a nice young lady in Buffalo and we wrote back and forth to each other for about a year and decided to get married. So after I was commissioned I sent a telegram to the commanding general of Mitchell Air Force Base and I said, "Request ten days delay en route to get married," and it came back "Five days granted." So I'm at Yale, I have got to get back to Buffalo, said, "Okay. We'll get married." Her own parents had died so she lived with my parents and made the arrangements, got married, had our honeymoon in downtown Buffalo at the Hotel Richford. I got home on a Friday, went to church on Sunday, got married on Monday, Tuesday night, and I had to report back Wednesday.

I reported back to Mitchell Air Force Base on Wednesday all by myself, and was assigned to Bradley Field, Connecticut; that's near Hartford. And then I sent for my bride. We got married in May of 1943 and she came up there within a few days and we lived in Hartford, Connecticut. A civilian drove me back and forth. I was in charge of a communications group and in September, 1943 we got orders to leave. She went down to the bus there and I kissed her goodbye, and finally I came back in December of '45.

Well, from the 322nd Fighter Control Squadron which was based at Bradley Field, Connecticut, we went down to Newport News, Virginia, and from there we were on the liberty ship that went overseas to Oran in North Africa.

Q: What was your first impression of the Rohna?

Schulz: I didn't know anything about ships. It looked all right to me. It's just another ship. The only interesting part about the trip over the Atlantic from the U.S. to North Africa was that there was a movie star on the ship, Sterling Hayden hung around with the Captain and what not. I also got acquainted with this Captain Hogan. We bunked together.

For the last 50, 60 years I've been telling everybody that on the way over from the U.S. to Oran somebody on the liberty ship had an attack of acute appendicitis and Captain Hogan was a doctor and he was older than me; I was 23 and he was 39. We got acquainted and he said, "I got to do this surgery," and "Do you want to help?" I said, "Yeah. Well, what can I do?" He said, "You can give the anesthetic." "Okay. And how will I do that?" And he said, "You'll hold this and put ether on it and so forth," and

Capt. Carlton P. Hogan, MD.

he also asked another fellow that was a second lieutenant; I can't think of his name; whether he'd help and there was just the three of us. The other fellow got sick watching the surgery and had to leave. There was just the two of us, and I said, "Did you ever do one of these surgeries before?" He said, "No, but I delivered a lot of babies. But I've watched, I've participated and assisted." Oh, I can remember another thing he said, "We are going to give him some nice, fancy stitches here." To make a long story short the guy walked off the ship. It was a very successful operation.

When we landed in Oran I traveled with him; they had better food and all that and we had quite a nice time.

Captain Hogan's niece came to the Rohna reunion for the first time and that I was able to tell her something about seeing him, helping him and everything. In all these years that these reunions have been going on I've got a stack of letters at home from people that have written me. I've got e-mails that said, "Did you know So and So?" I hadn't been able to help one person to say, "I remember him," except his niece today.

Q: Where were you when the attack began?

Schulz: I was on the third deck watching a card game and being the very dutiful husband that I was, newly married, I wasn't going to gamble nickels and dimes away but I was watching some friends of mine play poker when it all happened.

When the ship was hit it was all exciting. Don't forget, I was just 23 years old, very exciting. You'd see these tracer bullets all of a sudden going all over the place. I never saw an airplane, couldn't see them. I went from one side to the other with everybody else. And I really can say that I never saw an airplane, I never saw the glider bomb come in and hit the ship. I didn't know anything about it. I never felt the explosion. I know the ship was listing severely and I was on the low side and I knew enough to go on the high side and I watched people jumping, the pandemonium. There were no drills and no lifeboat drills or anything like that, and that's where I was.

Q: Where was Captain Hogan?

Schulz: Captain Hogan was just standing there on deck, talking to my friend. I talked to them and I said, "Don't you think we'd better go? I'm going to go." And that's when I went.

The bomb had exploded inside and blew out the side of the ship. I watched a lifeboat being lowered by crew members. They lowered it where it tilted and some of them fell out. I watched that lifeboat and when it hit the water and started floating away; that was when I decided that I was going to go overboard. I had my helmet on and I had my gun on and everything. I had my shoes on, my glasses, and my watch, and I just swung out and where the side of the ship blew out from the explosion it was like a platform, and I went down, swung on a rope, right down on to that, got my breath, hesitated, and then I swung out and dropped off into the water. And that was the lifeboat that I ultimately got into.

We didn't have life jackets; they were life belts. I knew you could squeeze them but I blew up one side, blew it up by air, and when I put it on apparently I only had the one side blown up 'cause I wound up without a life preserver and when I was picked up by the rescue ship, Clan Campbell, I didn't have a life preserver and I was frightened. I got into that lifeboat … I met one other person that was on that lifeboat just by accident. My wife ran into them as we were leaving one of the reunions. She just happened to ask, "Were any of you guys on a lifeboat?" And one said, "I was." She said, "My husband was too." He broke down. I don't even know who it was. The only person I have ever met that was on that lifeboat with me.

Q: About how many were on it? Do you remember?

Schulz: Packed, half full of water, people hanging on to the sides all around the whole thing, around the whole boat. I thought sure with all the water in it and the people and if anyone else was going to be climbing in that we'd lose the boat. I was concerned too about being close to the Rohna and I was fearful of being drawn in with it when it went under. While we were in the lifeboat the Rohna sunk just like that, just like you saw it do it in the movie "Titanic." It went down stern first until it disappeared but it was quite a sight.

In the meantime because all of the ammunition was going off as I remember tracer bullets, everything else, explosions going on, and fire. You could see the fire in the hull that I remember and I can still think of one funny thing. I'm bailing out and I got my helmet. There were some people wouldn't make a move. I'm a loud mouth and I'm not afraid. I'm sort of a take charge, bail out, and I'm bailing out and looking at some humorous things. A few times I'd throw it right in the face of somebody that was hanging on the side. In retrospect, it was sort of funny. And the funniest thing was I'm sitting there. I hear one young fellow, and I'm 23, a young fellow, we're all yelling. He said, "Listen to the lieutenant. Listen to the lieutenant." I don't know whether there were any other officers on that lifeboat because nobody else said anything or I didn't see anybody. I was sitting there right in the bow of the boat. I was saying, "Don't try to get in. Hold everybody on the side. Hold on to them. We're going to lose the boat." The Rohna went away, sunk, pitch dark and all of a sudden we see this great, big ship that we're drifting into and it was the Clan Campbell.

Q: What do you think the period of time was you were on the life-boat?

Schulz: I have no idea. I wish I had my watch but I threw it away. I'm guessing within a couple hours anyway from the time that I went over, was in the water, got on the boat, drifting around and that, but I have no idea.

Q: How did they get all of you off the lifeboat?

Schulz: Well, I realized with that with the heavy seas that the boat was going up maybe ten feet or more with the swells. Some people as soon as they got to the boat were scrambling and trying to get up the ropes and ladders. Some of them went off at the low swell. And mentally I said, "When I'm going off I'm going to wait until on the high swell," and I think I was about the third or fourth one left on the boat. I don't know who was left but I think they might have been hurt, traumatized or whatever, because they were still there when I went off. When I got up I didn't try to scramble up. I had my arms around those ropes there and I said, "I'm this far. I'm not going to fall off now." And when I got my leg over the top I was about halfway up the side of the Clan Campbell when I made my move, and when I got to the top I fell down. Then I got sick and threw up, and it was pitch black. I was wondering where everyone is and what happened to the men still on the lifeboat.

I thought, "Why aren't there people from the ship helping?" You read about the Pioneer. You hear these stories here that the guys are right there waiting to take you and lead you away and help you get up and everything. There wasn't a soul there. And then I opened up a door into the ship and I'm just opening up doors and I'm going into officers' quarters and looking through their stuff. I opened up a few doors and somebody came up and said, "What are you looking for? What are you here for?" I said, "I don't have a life preserver. I want a life preserver." He answered, "Don't worry about it. Follow me." And then took me where there were some other people that had been picked up sitting around, smoking, and I said, "Anybody got a dry cigarette?" Then they gave us dry clothes to wear.

Q: Where did the Clan Campbell take you at that point?

Schulz: Took it back in to Philippeville.

Q: What occurred after that time-wise once you were back in there?

Schulz: Well, I don't remember how long we were there. It was a tent city. We were in tents and I had free time because I went to some gin mills to get something to drink or what and I really don't know. I don't know how long we were in Philippeville. I don't know before we got on another ship. I have no idea.

Q: Where did you end up?

Schulz: The wonderful English people had put together survivor packages of sneakers and socks and shorts and slacks and T-shirts and stuff like that. So we had dry clothing and then we had to get military clothing. I know I had to put in a statement of charges as to what I paid for everything and they reimbursed me financially for all the clothes that I lost.

Well, anyway, we went back in to the Mediterranean, Suez Canal, Red Sea, Indian Ocean, Bombay, and then from Bombay we went by freight cars to Calcutta. In Calcutta I met a lieutenant Cole and he had gone by way of the Pacific with the 322nd Fighter Control radio equipment, all of the supplies and all that. And what was left of the 322nd Fighter Control or all the survivors, they went over in to China to Kunming and

Bill Cole and I were left behind in Calcutta to get the equipment. And I think we were there for a couple of weeks enjoying Calcutta. They had night life there. I remember the Great Eastern Hotel; there was a jazz band and stuff like that and so we enjoyed our stay in Calcutta before we went over the hump into Kunming, China.

I got there by first available transportation and I went down to find out who was going and then I wound up in a truck driven by a Chinese driver and it was the worst ride I've had in my life; sheer drops of hundreds of feet. They burned part alcohol and part gasoline and terrible fumes and I was very happy to arrive in Yunnanee after that trip along the Burma Road. I was then assigned to take over a radio station in Poashan China, and we bivouacked in a pagoda, with an emergency landing strip. From Poashan, China, I had a group there. I went to another place in French Indochina, which is now Vietnam, called Mengtse. There I had a C47 drop me off with all of our equipment, some tents, hundred-gallon barrels of gasoline for refueling with an emergency landing strip and in the middle of nowhere. I got acquainted with some Chinese generals there, and through them they had their coolies come in and they built us barracks out of bamboo and straw. We had people that would come in, needed gas or they had some problem. They'd stay overnight.

I was a first lieutenant then and I got a cook from the Chinese and he built a stove out of mud and what not. I bought a couple of chickens and we had fresh eggs every day. Of course, being the ranking officer I got the first one and we switched off on the eggs. And then the Chinese general said, "I'm going to give you a pig" and they gave us a little pig. What are we going to do with a pig? We built a little corral and fed him. We had an emergency landing there and a guy came in and he said, "I'll fix it. I can slaughter that. I know all about it." So the only shot that I fired during all of World War II besides in practice was that pig. I shot the pig dead and he skinned him and we had meat and we had it salted. He showed us what to do with it. We had some fresh meat for a while.

There was a Catholic bishop there and I was introduced to him and he was saying, "Gee. I haven't seen any of my priests in so long." And I said, "Well, where they?" He showed me on the map and I said, "Well, I've got a spot right down here. I'll get some provisions for you and you can fly down with me," and I went around and collected stuff from food, K-rations, C-rations, cigarettes, everything else, and clothing that people didn't want. So I flew him down there and then I introduced him to the general that I had become acquainted with. He got horses for him, put on a pack horse. He was Chinese but I had studied for the priesthood and I had about seven years of Latin behind me, so we could get by talking Latin.

I had one other assignment in Mengtse and that's where we heard the atom bomb was dropped and that was when we got ready to go back.

We went around by the Atlantic, Red Sea, Indian Ocean, come back by way of the Pacific, Tacoma, Washington. We stopped in there and I got off the train with Bill Cole, and there was a gin mill right up the road a block and I said, "Come on." They said, "This thing isn't going to leave for a while." We're going out and enjoying a beer and the train takes off. Oh, my God, we're going to be court martialed! But we made it back. We hadn't seen our wives in almost three years, so we called them up and had them meet us in New York City. Our two wives met us and we spent a week in New York and got reacquainted and then came back and that's the end of the story.

LEON JOSEPH STASIAK
Rohna Casualty

By Johna D'Angelo, Jr.

Leon (Leo) Joseph Stasiak was born on August 6, 1922 in Elm Park, Staten Island, NY. His parents were Albert and Fanny and he was the youngest of four children. Leo attended St. Albert's Catholic Church and school. He grew up fast, strong, intelligent, handsome and brave.

Shortly before Christmas, 1942 he received a letter to report for active duty and entered the service on January 25, 1943. He was in the 853rd Engineer BN. His best friends were Joe Trapanese from Staten Island and Walter Stankiewicz from Long Island. The three were inseparable until the sinking of the Rohna. Joe and Walter survived, Leo did not.

I have communicated with Joe by phone and mail and met with Frank Stankiewicz (Walter's nephew) at the Rohna reunion in Washington, DC in 2004. We did not know each other and happened to sit at the same table. Frank told me that his uncle Walter had often spoken about this corker of a Polack from Staten Island who was killed. But Frank did not know his name until we met and shared photos.

When I was a little boy I remember seeing a picture of a young man in an Army uniform hanging over the mantel at my grandparent's house. My mother told me that he was my Uncle Leo and had died in WWII when the ship he was on was torpedoed off North Africa.

In 1993 on the 50th anniversary of his death I decided to investigate his military record. Nobody in my family even knew what outfit he was in. I thought it would be easy because I had his name, address and service number. I sent for information, but each time I was answered (sometimes not answered at all), I was told that his records were lost, misplaced or burned in a fire. One reply even said that he was never in the Army at all!

In 1998, my wife and I went to the National Archives in Washington, DC and were told the same old story. A lady asked me for my address. One day in December of 2001, I received an unmarked package. In it was everything about Leo and the Rohna. I was totally shocked!

All my life I had been a WWII buff and had never heard of the Rohna. A friend found the website and I made contact with John Fievet who has been a great help and has become a close friend. Jim Bennett, Carl Schoenacker and Bob Brewer have helped me find men who knew Uncle Leo. I've been in communication with Henry Kuberski and Ken Gerrard who knew my uncle.

On October 25, 2002 Leo finally received a beautiful ceremony at Arlington cemetery. I had written a letter to the superintendent of the cemetery and had asked how I could arrange a funeral. Ten days later he replied that my story was amazing but he needed proof since he could not find any information about the Rohna. I made copies and sent them off to him.

In June of 2007 the street my uncle grew up on (Pulaski Ave) was renamed Pvt. Leon J. Stasiak Ave. He is also enrolled in the WWII memorial honor roll, The Washington National Cathedral Purple Heart Museum and the US Army museum.

AN INTERVIEW WITH S.E. WAGGONER

USS Pioneer, AM 105

Edited for readability

Waggoner: After I was commissioned I had several assignments in the States and was eventually assigned to the Pioneer. I knew Ron Wright quite well. He was a quartermaster there and, truthfully, I think he knew everyone on the ship.

Q: Tell me a little bit about your trip from the U.S. over to the Mediterranean.

Waggoner: We did escort duty there a number of trips across, to and from the Mediterranean back to the States escorting troops. We did it until the invasion of Italy and, when we went into Italy, we only swept two times the entire time I was on the Pioneer. The remainder of the time, we did escort duty. But, anyway, we swept and just made one trip with the Pioneer out in the deeper waters and small YMS's swept in close then and we just dropped back out and started doing patrol duty on both Italy and Southern France. It was only two times we had our sweeping gear in the water. Remaining time was doing nothing but patrol.

Q: Let's back up a little bit and talk about the Rohna incident itself on the 26th of November, 1943 when you were doing escort duty.

Waggoner: We were assigned to an English squadron command for that trip. We were working out of Bizerte and I shall never forget. We were on the left quarter of the convoy. We had recently received the equipment where we could take control of the radio controlled bombs from the German planes. See, those planes, as you're aware, stayed off by 20-something miles from the convoy and guided those bombs, which looked like little small airplanes. I don't know if you ever saw one. The first time we saw them it was before and I said, "Oh, look, Captain," I was on the flying bridge with the captain during the whole general quarters, and I said, "Look, they got one of our planes coming straight for us." He looked at it and he said, "You look at that again. That's one of those radio-controlled bombs that we've been hearing about." It was that one that sunk the transport (HMT Rohna) there that particular evening. And we were in a position that we picked up the majority of the survivors that was picked up. And we stayed there and picked them up. It got dark and the captain says, "Put floodlights out here on the water and disregard the security hazard of being spotted." So we did and we continued picking up survivors after dark. We left, I don't remember exactly the time, but it was after dark and got back with 606 survivors and 600 of them were living, six dead onboard. And you couldn't get in the hold; both decks were full of people. We were trying to get them a little hot coffee and a little food and something while the C.O. of the convoy there said, "Carry them back to Bizerte".

Q: Tell me about the Quartermaster, Ron Wright.

Waggoner: Ron Wright was a very capable individual. His assignment in general quarters was steering the ship. He more or less was in charge of the wheelhouse and steering the ship and the speeds. And in general quarters there, he was in charge there and he was steering it and regulating the speed of the ship, trying to keep it where the survivors were and that was his responsibility.

Q: What was Captain Rodgers like?

Waggoner: Well, now, he was a gentleman if I've ever seen one, very capable individual. As I referred to, I was saying a plane was coming in, he said, "No," he was very knowledgeable, he said, "That's the bomb that they've developed." And he was very, very knowledgeable and calm individual and gentleman if I've ever seen one.

Q: Do you remember what orders he gave when the bombers were spotted? What happened on the ship?

Waggoner: Well, yes, when we determined that they were radio bombs, he says, "Stop shooting at the plane; put nothing but a line of smoke between the bomb and the planes off in the distance." So we just put up a barrage of smoke bombs and have them explode so hopefully the planes could not track the bomb on in.

Q: Do you remember what he did so he could maximize how many survivors you picked up? What he did with the ship?

Waggoner: Oh, we just laid to. We laid to in the water and disregarded the planes that were coming in. See, there were three or four bombs that they were aimed at us and they picked us up out of the water but we lay to and picked up survivors and our crew was in the water pulling the men up to the ship. That was the busiest day I had in the Navy was that evening and night, trying to keep all those soldiers below deck. I was down there just making the soldiers get out of the way because they were on the deck, in the way of our sailors pulling men on board and that was my responsibility during that recovery.

Q: Okay. Tell me a little bit about what you saw the Pioneer guys doing.

Waggoner: We had to watch them to keep them from over exerting themselves, going in the water, pulling people up to the ship, getting them on board. They disregarded their safety to rescue those survivors.

Q: Your ship had a crew of about 100. And you pulled 600 guys in. Where did you put them?

Waggoner: Well, we put them down in the hold. On deck, anywhere they could find a spot to put one. We just crammed them in holds, in the hatches going down to the holds and they'd get down in there and stay there.

Q: I understand that some of the men that the Pioneer rescued were injured very badly.

Waggoner: Oh, yeah. We had our medical crew on the ship; they were examining the ones that were injured, yes.

Q: I've also heard that, during a lot of the action, the guns were just firing like crazy, you know, off your ship, anti-aircraft and whatever else you had. Do you remember any of that?

Waggoner: Well, we tried to not just be firing. We stopped shooting at planes and started putting a barrage up between the airplane and the bomb; we were very lucky on the Pioneer. I believe it was two or three of our sailors got shrapnel, from near misses, nothing critical. Just before I left the ship and we got back to the States, it had been put in dry dock and, between each rib, that hull was bent in. It was from those bombs, we were picked up out of the water a number of times. Our speed had been reduced quite radically because of the washboard effect going through the water.

Q: Do you remember any particular other men aboard the ship?

Waggoner: I remember Clyde Bellamy he got to be chief but I think he was first class, gunner's mate there when I was on the Pioneer. He was a very capable individual. I shall never forget ... He said, "I've got a little present for you." And just before I left the ship, he gave me a scabbard and a knife that he'd made altogether and I still got that. It's there at home now. I told my son, I said, "You keep this knife now; it's a hunting knife is what it is; and you keep this knife in remembrance of your old man."

Q: I've seen pictures of the Pioneer. There isn't a lot of deck. I mean, it's covered with big reels and lots of stuff so I imagine you had to keep that deck pretty clear.

Waggoner: I was on the main deck, trying to keep order, getting those survivors over the rails and into the hold. I guess it was eight or ten feet from the wide there up and down, the forward part of the ship had quite a bit of flat deck, but you couldn't reach the water from there. The main deck, we had ladders thrown over the rail on the ship and the survivors that were capable, they would crawl up that ladder and the ones that were not capable, we would get them on board some way, either put a rope around them or somebody would crawl up that ladder and bring them up.

Q: How many Pioneer men were doing the rescue? Physically pulling the guys aboard?

Waggoner: Oh, I guess 40 or 50. Everyone who was not in direct need to be at a station was there pulling them in; either in the water or on the deck. And on deck there was quite a few that were pulling them up and I'll never forget that. They went up on the gun deck there and got them out of the way and the medics were working on them up there. Oh, it was the darndest rat race you've ever seen in your life that night.

Q: Some of the Rohna survivors have nothing but praise for you guys.

Waggoner: Well, I'll tell you, I think they did an outstanding job, our crew. They were very determined to get the survivors onboard and, when we had to leave that night, our men were still in the water. We had to be sure we got all our crew back onboard

AN INTERVIEW WITH AARON WEBER

Rohna Survivor

Edited for readability

Weber: I enlisted on July 23, 1942. And after being inducted in Maryland, I took my basic training at Camp Wheeler, Georgia. Now, Camp Wheeler, Georgia at that time, was infantry training. So I had basic infantry training. And then, they transferred me to an Air Force station in Manchester, New Hampshire, which there was an Army airfield. I was there around six months, sort of, doing M.P. duty. After that, they asked me if I wanted to go to radio school, and I did. I wanted to get out of New Hampshire because it was very  cold there in the winter of 1942. Well, anyway, I landed in Sioux Falls, South Dakota, and spent from March until July going to school there, learning the mechanics of radio and Morse code. Next I got a telegram saying I had been transferred to an outfit in Connecticut. I guess it was a place where soldiers were being assigned to various outfits. They assigned me to the 322nd Fighter Control Squadron, when I got there and I saw them packing up to go overseas. We went down to Newport News, Virginia, where we shipped out, which took us around 20 days to Oran, North Africa. And that's where we landed in a small town right near Oran, North Africa.

Oh, it was miserable there. When we came in, it was raining. We had to pitch tents and the water was streaked with oil. I woke up during the night, and I was almost floating away. We hadn't had time to dig a little moat around the tent. But otherwise, somehow, we got through. Somebody says, "Let's get some wine." So the guy went and got the wine. Only, he got it in one of those five-gallon gasoline containers. And there must've been some gasoline left in there. So we were drinking wine with a gasoline kicker. Well, anyway, after about three weeks in North Africa we got onto the Rohna.

Q: What was your first impression of the Rohna?

Weber: It looked like a dumpy old ship. There was still a lot of rust on there. But I didn't know any better. You know, nobody else did, either. We didn't know anything about being attacked or things like that. And we spent Thanksgiving Day, I think, when we got on the ship and then, left that port in North Africa. And a day later is when we were attacked.

Q: Where were you during the attack?

Weber: I was down below, playing cards with some other fellows. Oh, I remember playing Knock Rummy or some game like that. And I was the only person to survive of that group of five. And it's a funny thing, just today, one of the fellows I was playing cards with, a fellow named John Tilberg (Tilberg, John B., T/Sgt., 32579570, AC), who I thought, and I think, had come from Buffalo. I wasn't 100 percent sure. So just today, I looked in the Buffalo telephone book, and I couldn't find the name Tilberg at all. And when the attack started, we, sort of, got up and separated. And I never saw any of those fellows again. Well, I know one fellow's name was Javorsky. And another fellow, he was an Irish fellow, I can't think of his name. But the four of them and I were playing cards and that's when the attack took place.

Q: Describe the attack.

Weber: Well, we heard a lot of guns going off, machine guns and anti-aircraft guns and I didn't know what was going on. We were down below. And all I knew is what people told me afterwards what transpired up on deck. They told us to stay below deck. And finally, we heard them say, "Get up onto the deck and abandon ship." And the first thing I saw when I got out of the doorway was Captain Hogan, (Hogan, Carlton P., Cap't, 0-1688092, AC) from Burlington, New Jersey. And his granddaughter's here now for the reunion in Buffalo. Anyway, I saw him administering first aid to a group of G.I.'s. And I just glanced his way, and I went on to see what was going on. I was in the dark about what was really going on, and I was all by myself. And they keep saying you had to abandon ship. And I felt the ship had tilted. It was sort of on a slant.

I did things automatically without thinking. For instance, I took off my shoes and arranged them in a nice pile, you know. And then, I took my life preserver. You're supposed to press carbon dioxide pellets and it would inflate. I didn't do that. You had the alternative to do it by mouth. And I blew up my life preserver, and I think I did a wise thing. Because it was loose, so when I went overboard and jumped from the ship, you know, I landed in the water. And then, I raised up and surfaced. And the life preserver was right where it should be, right under my armpits. Because I saw, at least two bodies floating in the water with their rear ends sticking up. They had inflated their belt using these pellets, or whatever you call them. And it was real tight around their waist, and they never raised it up to get under their armpits. And they were floating with their rear end up and their face in the water. And I turned around, noticing them, and I saw the Rohna with a big gaping red hole in the mid-section or thereabouts.

The first thing I did was holler for help. And I looked around. Who's going to help me? Everybody was in the same situation. And I, sort of, drifted to three other fellows. Now, one fellow, a young boy, could've been no more than 18 or 19, but he was floating with the water over his nose; so he was already dead. And I was an old man of 22. And another fellow was a British sailor. And he, sort of, looked in bad shape, and he drifted away. And then, there was the two of us, and I wasn't holding onto him. But he must have been holding onto me, holding onto my fatigue jacket. It started to turn dark and we kept looking around for somebody to save us. I couldn't see any ships, like people saw the Pioneer. I didn't see anything and it was dark already. It was a clear night, and the stars played a little trick on us. We were thinking we were seeing a light from a ship, when it was actually a star, one of the brighter stars. But finally, after seven to eight hours, we were floating in the water that long. The only thing I said to this guy I was with, I said, "Where are you from?" He says, "Brooklyn." And that was the end of our conversation. I was more eager to look around to see how somebody could save us.

Finally, a boat, sort of a large row boat, loomed right in front of us and picked us up and took us to their ship, which was the HMS Holcomb. I think it was a British Corvette or small destroyer was the size of it. And when I got on, they took me down the deck and started to clean me up. Both of us had been floating in oil. And the funny thing is the oil had gotten into my hair. And it took, at least, three months before I got rid of all the oil from that.

I didn't realize that when they cleaned my face off, they were using those rags and stuff like that, I must've been hit by some debris, because I was bleeding around the chin. So they took me to the British hospital in a place called Bougie. And they just put something on there, and I went to the camp. I think, we were in a British camp, I can't remember the name of the outfit that was stationed there. It was a division of British troops, the ones with the high furry hats. Well, anyway, they do guard duty for the King and Queen of England and all that kind of stuff.

We were there around two or three days in this British Camp. You know, and I remember at four o'clock a truck came to where we were and brought us tea. And the first time I ever had tea with milk in it. You know, I'm more used to having tea plain. I'm not used to milk in it. But it didn't taste too bad. Well, anyway, after three days, we got on a 40 and 8 train car. That's 40 men or 8 horses, take your pick. It took us three days or two nights or something like that. I just don't remember. But it was, at least, two days. We traveled along this railroad. And we got to Bizerte and there's where we met with the rest of our outfit. Because the HMS Holcomb didn't land us as the Pioneer did. And that was it. And I found out who was missing and who didn't make it, you know.

Q: Did you have some good friends that didn't make it?

Weber: Since I just joined the outfit as they were packing I didn't have a chance to meet too many people. I met the company clerk, you would call. He was a Sergeant, fellow named Seidel, (Seidel, Max H., S/Sgt., 37415141, AC) who didn't make it. But I wasn't a friend of his. I just met him. But in fact, his sister was in Washington at our reunion. And she wanted to know what happened to her brother. And all I could tell her was that our site, where we were stationed on the Rohna, we were not hit by the bomb. It was hit some other place where, I think, the engineers were. And I tried to tell her that he, probably, drowned somehow.

And well, I made friends afterwards, you know. In fact, in Washington, there's a fellow here named Art Tomasino (Tomasino, Arthur A- 322nd Fighter Control Sqdn), who I was with in a place in China, which was near Burma and on the Burma road in China. And Washington, at the reunion, I didn't know he was there and he didn't know I was there. And you know Carl Schoenacker? He got on the microphone and he said, "We have here two guys that haven't seen each other in 60 years." And it turned out this was Art and myself. I thought he was reprimanding me for something when he mentioned my name. But I had one fellow, Ed Ashley, lived very close to me. We were together in China for a short period of time. But he's the one that told me about the Rohna Reunion Organization. He passed away a couple of years ago.

Q: Did you spend the rest of your service time in China?

Weber: Yes, until the war ended. It was a funny thing; I was transferred to Kunming around July of 1945, from Paushan. And I was working a radio station, which was situated in the middle of a Chinese cemetery. And I was monitoring the radio, and I heard the war was over. And I called headquarters, and I told them the war's over. And half an hour or an hour later, guns started to pop all around me. And I had a machine gun in that hut, that radio shack, and I sprayed the roof with it, just to see if it would work. I never shot the gun before. But then, it was time for me to leave and my replacement came. I, sort of, left that cemetery hunched over, because there were guns being fired all over the place. And I got back to the hostel okay. And then, after that it was just a time to wait for going back home.

Q: Talk about Captain Hogan.

Weber: Well, all I know, I spoke to Captain Hogan. He came from Burlington County, New Jersey, and I had a brother who had a business there in Burlington City. So it probably was on the Gilman going from Newport News to Oran that I asked him if he knew my brother. That was all. And he said, "No." That's the only time I ever spoke to him.

And the last time I saw him, actually, was when I saw him administering first aid. That was my entire experience with Captain Hogan. I had heard that on the Gilman, which was the liberty ship, from Newport News to Oran, that he performed an appendectomy operation on a fellow onboard ship, going to Oran. And somebody told me, recently, here, that that fellow, although recovered from the operation, never made it off the Rohna. So that was my experience with Captain Hogan.

I spoke recently, at a dedication in Camden, New Jersey, of the ones that didn't survive the Rohna, who resided in South Jersey. And Captain Hogan was one of them who they mentioned. And then, I got a letter from one of his nieces, and I told her what I knew about her uncle. And then, recently, another niece called me and I told her the same thing. And she's here today at the reunion in Buffalo, NY visiting us.

Q: In terms of your own life and the experience of having gone through the Rohna, did it make changes in your life?

Weber: I never spoke to anybody about it after I got back. I had friends, old friends from pre-war time and new friends. And I never spoke about it. I just said I was in China and doing radio work and that was it. And I never spoke too much to my wife about it. I told her about the ship, you know, but that was it. I'm not much of a speaker. I don't talk a lot. And it wasn't until I learned about the Rohna organization through, I think, Ed Ashley who passed away. And I went to the first reunion in San Antonio, Texas. And there I met other people who I didn't even know from my outfit. And you know, every year, now, I've been going and enjoying it and talking a lot with the other fellows. And that was that

Report of Rohna Second Officer: J.E. Wills

CONFIDENTIAL

MG.
T.D./139/1985.
17th December, 1943.

SHIPPING CASUALTIES SECTION—TRADE DIVISION
REPORT OF AN INTERVIEW WITH THE 2ND OFFICER, MR. J.E. WILLS
s.s. ROHNA—8,602 gross tons

Convoy K.M.F. 26
Sunk by 1 Glider Bomb from
enemy aircraft on the
26th November, 1943.

All times are B.S.T.
—1 hour for G.M.T.

Mr. Wills:

1. We were bound from Oran to Port Said, loaded with approximately 2,000 troops and their equipment. The ship was armed with 1–4", 1–2 pdr., 6 Oerlikons, 2 Hotchkiss, 2 twin Lewis, 1 Pillar Box, 4 F.A.M.S., and 2 P.A.C. Rockets. The crew numbered approximately 218, including 16 Naval and 2 Army Gunners; the troops were Americans with 3 British Army Medical Officers, and 10 Ranks. I do not know the number of casualties amongst either the crew or passengers, but 800 survivors were landed in Philippeville, and oth-

ers were probably landed elsewhere. All Confidential books, including the Wireless codes, were thrown overboard in a weighted box. Degaussing was on.

2. We sailed from Oran at 1230 on the 25th November, in company with four other ships, and at 1530 joined the main portion of convoy K.M.F. 26, taking up position No. 12, the 2nd ship of the port column. The convoy consisted of approximately 24 ships, formed in 6 columns, there being 4 ships in my column, escorted by 7/8 Destroyers.

3. No warnings of enemy aircraft being in the vicinity were received, and the convoy proceeded without incident until the 26th November. I came off the bridge at 1620 and went to my cabin for tea; about 10 minutes later I thought I hear gun-fire. I hurried to the bridge and had just arrived there when I saw a splash in the water, about 100 feet from the stern of the anti-aircraft cruiser H.M.S. COVENTRY. The COVENTRY was at this time ahead of the centre of the convoy, off our starboard bow, and when I saw her she was sheering away to port to where the Destroyer ATHERSTONE was stationed. Extra 2nd officer rang the alarm bells, and everyone we to "action stations." For the next forty minutes there were enemy aircraft constantly in sight, and I learned later that about 30 Heinkels 177 took part in the attack. They kept out of range of the gun-fire and appeared to be attacking the escorts. I saw several glider bombs released, one of which fell near the BANFORA, No. 14, last ship of my column, and I heard later that the Destroyer ATHERSTONE had five near-misses; luckily no damage was done to either of these vessels. At this time I did not know anything about these glider bombs, to me they appeared to be British fighters attacking the bombers and being shot down. When a glider bomb is first released it appears to fall behind the bomber, it then quickly overtakes it; a red glow appears

in the nose of the bomb, which then shoots downwards. I saw 3 or 4 "fighters" shot down in the course of the first hour of this attack.

4. The convoy did not alter course or reduce speed. The enemy planes continued skirting the convoy, making direct attacks on the escorts, and I learned later that a torpedo attack was also made on the convoy; their intention was apparently to cripple the escorts before attacking the merchant ships. I also learned that the reason we did not receive a warning of the impending attack was because the enemy had jammed the radio location apparatus.

5. Shortly after 1700 several other enemy aircraft appeared, and at one time I saw four in formation off the port quarter. The escort's gunfire however appeared to be keeping the planes from attacking. At 1725 on the 26th November I observed two bombers approaching the ship from the port quarter, flying at a height of approximately 3,000 feet. One of them attacked the ship ahead, the other, when he was just abeam of us, swerved toward us and launched a bomb from about 2 points before the beam. At this time we were 15 miles N. from Jijelli, North Africa, steering 100 (degrees) (approx.) at 12 knots. The weather was fine and cloudy, the sun was setting and visibility good; there was a moderate sea with a long swell, and N.W'ly wind, force 3.

6. When first released the bomb appeared to be a little below and to the starboard of the plane, it then closed the plane, shot downwards, swerving to the right of the plane, and a red glow appeared in its nose. When it was half way I realized that it was a glider bomb; I gave orders for the port Oerlikon to open fire, which order was carried out, but I do not think any hits were scored. The bomb struck the ship in the engine room, on the port side, just above the water line. There was not a loud explosion; in fact the near-miss explosions were far more

violent. The engine room flooded immediately and caught fire, all electrical equipment failed. No. 4 bulkhead collapsed, and the Radio Officer, who was on the boat deck at the time, said that a large quantity of debris, soldier's kit, tin hats, etc., was thrown into the air, one of the troop decks being abaft No. 4 bulkhead. The vessel listed slightly to starboard; the shell plates about 6 ft. above the water level on both the port and starboard sides were blown outwards and upwards. I went to the boat deck and released the belly bands from the boats, then returned to the Bridge for orders. The Master decided that nothing could be done and ordered "abandon ship," so I returned to the boat deck. The ship carried 22 lifeboats, 14 swung outboard and 8 stowed inboard; 4 of the outboard and 2 inboard boats were smashed by the explosion and were therefore useless. The falls of several of the forward lifeboats were cut by the troops; consequently the boats fell into the water and became waterlogged. A number of the boats could not be lowered as the falls had become jammed, and eventually only eight lifeboats were lowered, most of which capsized or filled with water on becoming airborne. The Chief and 3rd Engineers managed to lower No. 10 Fleming lifeboat successfully. Many of the troops, being unaccustomed to the ship, became slightly panicky and also there was a fairly rough sea running. The Chief Officer, who was Troops Officer, had held a boat drill so there should have been no confusion as everyone should have known his boat station.

7. By this time the vessel had listed 12 degrees to starboard, so we threw the rafts overboard, helped by the troops and the D.E.M.S. gunners. The ship carried 101 rafts, practically all of which were released, and most of the crew and troops abandoned ship on them. By 1750 only 50 troops remained on the fore deck; as there were no more rafts they threw hatch boards over the side from No. 3 hatch, using them as rafts. The fire in the engine room quickly spread and smoke and flames were pouring from No. 4 hold. H.M. Destroyer

ATHERSTONE and an American minesweeper dropped behind the convoy, and the ATHERSTONE laid a smoke screen.

8. None of the troops had red lights on their lifebelts, and although there were two or three vessels searching for survivors, it was very difficult to see them in the water, as it was getting dark. Eventually all the troops and crew were clear of the ship, with the exception of myself, the Master, Chief and 3rd Officers, the S.M.O. and 4 American soldiers. We remained on the fore deck for about half an hour after the rest of the men had left. The S.M.O. complained about his hand, which was badly burned, so the Chief Officer went to the boat deck to collect a first aid kit from one of the damaged boats. Whilst he was doing so there was a peculiar rending noise, clouds of smoke belched from No. 3 hold, and the vessel settled rapidly by the stern. We hastily threw the four remaining rafts overboard, I jumped after them, and swam a few strokes away from the vessel; when I turned round again the ship's bows were just disappearing; she finally sank about 1 ½ hours after the bomb had struck.

9. I heard later that the Master was rescued, but I do not think that the Chief Officer managed to escape; he would have been on the boat deck when the vessel sank, and unless he jumped overboard immediately, he would certainly have been dragged under. The S.M.O. is also missing, but the 3rd Officer and the 4 Americans were all picked up.

10. After being nearly an hour in the water, I was picked up by the H.M. Destroyer ATHERSTONE.

11. I think there were a great number of troops killed in the initial explosion as No. 4 'tween deck was No. 7 troop deck, and at least 320 troops were accommodated there. Of the D.E.M.S. gunners, Petty Officer

Keegan, in charge of the 12 pdr. forward, is the only man missing from the 12 pdr. crew. The crews of the 12 pdr. and Pillar Box put up a very good barrage, which certainly turned away at least one enemy plane, even if they did not actually hit it. I do not know anything about the other gunners, except that Gunner Harrison was badly wounded, and I saw Gunner Thompson on shore later. On first sighting the enemy aircraft we opened fire with everything except the 4", the P.A.C.s and the F.A.M.S., the 12 pdr. crew firing about 20 rounds. I learned that the Destroyer ATHERSTONE fired about 650 rounds of 4".

12. No. 1 Deck Serang Bhowan Meetha did outstandingly fine work in his efforts to get the boats away. He went about in a perfectly cool, calm manner, and rendered valuable assistance to the Chief Officer throughout. His face was badly burned, and on landing at Philippeville on the 27th November, he was taken to Hospital. Naval Gunner Keegan, P.O., was also outstanding. He kept his 12 pdr. in action during the attack and afterwards saw all his gun' crew away safely and did everything possible for their safety.

13. I consider that parties of about 12 troops in charge of an officer, should be stationed in various parts of the ship and be detailed for emergency duties. Our Native crew, on this occasion, filled and lowered the two after lifeboats whilst the ship still had considerable weigh, without orders. Had there been an emergency party present, this would have been stopped, and the natives made to assist in lowering the lifeboats. As it was, except for the No. 1 Deck Serang, none of the native crew did anything to assist in lowering the lifeboats.

14. Whilst on board H.M. Destroyer ATHERSTONE I was informed by the Gunnery Officer that, as one of the glider bombs passed over their vessel, black grease issued from its tail, and the faces of several of the crew were bespattered with it.

Story of the Rohna Memorial

By John P. Fievet

At long last, a Rohna Memorial! It has been said that we can now put to rest the memory of our friends and loved ones who died on the Rohna. A monument of granite and bronze should withstand the ravages of time to serve as a reminder of the supreme sacrifice the 1,015 young men made to assure that future generations might live their lives in freedom.

The idea of a memorial to our comrades who died on the Rohna was born when James C. Blaine, who lost his brother Frank on the Rohna, sent me a clipping dated October 25, 1994 out of the Los Angeles Times giving details of a memorial being dedicated at Fort Rosecrans National Cemetery in San Diego to 126 men who died on the St. Lo; the first American ship to be sunk by a Kamikaze pilot. I learned from Rosecrans Cemetery that the Department of Veterans Affairs in Washington D.C. would have to be contacted for the procedure for placing a monument in a national cemetery. In November 1994 I wrote to both the Department of Veterans Affairs and Arlington Cemetery requesting information. I received a very enthusiastic reply from the Department of Veterans Affairs stating that they were honored that we were considering a National Cemetery as a location to memorialize the men who died on the Rohna. Arlington responded with a "ho-hum" reply saying that we would be permitted to plant a tree and place a 12 x 18 inch marker in Arlington. At that point, I decided to pursue a memorial through the Department of Veterans Affairs. Incidentally, a subsequent letter to Arlington asking if it would be possible to place a memorial in a national cemetery was never answered.

I found that as a survivor I could not request a group memorial in a national cemetery. I then contacted Jim Blaine and he graciously consented to make the formal request which was accepted by the National Cemetery Director on February 25, 1995. The next step was to choose a location and formulate a plan to fund the project. When the question of location was put to Jim Blaine, he said "it's your project, put it where you want to". At that time, I was aware that my physical condition wasn't what it used to be, so in June 1995 I decided to check a cemetery in Alabama. I made a three hour trip to Fort Mitchell and was impressed with the beauty of the cemetery and the reception of the Director. With concurrence of Jim and Ruth Canney, it was decided that the monument would be located at Fort Mitchell. The design of the monument was predetermined by the Department of Veterans Affairs since it had to match existing monuments. Now that I had a location and a monument design, the next question was how to finance the project. The Reunion in May 1995 in Columbus, Ohio gave us the answer. The only proper course was to make this memorial an exclusive endeavor of survivors, next-of-kin and Pioneer crewmen. Competitive bids were obtained on the monument using government specifications and a monetary fundraising goal was set. A fundraising letter was sent to names on Ruth Canney's roster of those attending the 1993 and 1995 reunions.

In October 1995, sufficient funds were available to purchase the monument and a proposal was submitted for approval to the Director at Fort Mitchell. Previously, it was suggested by the Department of Veterans Affairs that the sponsorship of the memorial be channeled through an established Veterans Organization. Since Veterans Organizations had not been especially helpful in furthering the interest in the Rohna tragedy, I requested and got approval to form our own organization: thus, the Rohna Survivors Memorial Organization came to be. On November 7, 1995 our proposal, meeting all government requirements, was submitted to Fort Mitchell and final approval was received on December 4, 1995. Order for the monument was placed on December 6, 1995.

We had the option of having our own private ceremony or have the dedication on Memorial Day May 30, 1996. Since we would have the pomp and ceremony that went along with the scheduled Memorial Day celebration, the Organization

REMEMBER THE ROHNA

DEDICATED TO THE MEMORY OF
THE 1,015 MEN WHO DIED IN WORLD WAR II
WHEN THE HMT ROHNA WAS SUNK
BY A GUIDED MISSILE LAUNCHED FROM A
GERMAN BOMBER ON NOVEMBER 26, 1943.
MAY THEY REST IN PEACE.
THE ROHNA SURVIVORS MEMORIAL ASSOCIATION
MAY 30, 1996

elected to dedicate our monument on Memorial Day. Someone suggested that we might make this event a mini-reunion, so I contacted the Columbus Convention Center for their recommendation of a site to accommodate our group. All contributors were notified the date of the ceremony and asked to advise if they planned to attend. In early February 1996 I found that my physical problem was not just old age but a heart problem that demanded immediate attention. Consequently triple bypass surgery as performed on February 26th. I have been blessed with many special friends in my life and when I needed one the most Carl Schoenacker came to the rescue. He didn't miss a beat and took over the job of lining up a place to have the mini-reunion and also planned a delightful dinner on the eve of the dedication. Our thanks go to Carl and Gus Gikas for arriving a day early and scouting out the best route to the cemetery. Also a special thanks to Ruth Canney for presiding over the Hospitality Room.

I'm certain that most of you are aware that the first book to be published on the Rohna disaster will be published in November. The book entitled "The Forgotten Tragedy" was written by Carlton Jackson, history professor at Western Kentucky University is being published by the Naval Institute Press. Carlton learned of the Rohna when he read an article in the Louisville Courier that came out of Birmingham on November 10, 1994. If you have trouble in locating the book, please don't hesitate to contact me. Copies of the dedication of the monument and acceptance by the Fort Mitchell Director are available as are copies of the speeches by officers of the Rohna Survivors Memorial Organization.

To all of you who attended the ceremony and to those who couldn't attend but contributed to the cost of the monument, we extend our sincere thanks. We will never forget you and will always be grateful.

James Blaine's Speech

At the dedication of the Rohna Memorial 5/30/1996

It is my pleasure and honor to represent the families who received "next of kin" letters for loved ones lost on the Rohna.

When I was asked to speak on behalf of such a large group, I asked myself, "where do I begin?" ... "where do I end?" I am sure, however, you have had many of the same feelings as I, and can say many, if not all of the things I hope to say in memory of our loved ones; be they our "brothers," "fathers," "uncles".

Fifty three years is a long time, but we remember the way they looked, talked, responded ... yes, those many years ago! Although we too have changed, we do not feel old, although the eyes fail, the ears grow dull, the words stumble, the mind fades, but thankfully, the heart remembers!

Even as we recall the memories of our loved ones, these memories also grow older. The sharp pain of loss becomes a dull ache. The emptiness, once so dark and deep, has been "crowded out" from the "day to day", but the sense of loss is still there and Memorial Day brings back memories of our loved ones ... their smiles, their looks, their laughs, their love, their dreams.

So we gather today to honor and dedicate this memorial to the 1,015 loved ones who died in the sinking of the Rohna, November 26, 1943.

Many years ago, an unknown poet wrote:

"In a sense, there is no death. The life of a person on earth lasts beyond his departure. You will always feel that life touching yours … that voice speaking to you in the familiar things he loved, he worked with, he touched. He lives on in your life and in the lives of all who knew him."

So, let us think of our loved ones today. Let us carry their courage forward. Let us be thankful that we can gather today and pause … just to remember.

God bless you and yours and rest in peace, dear loved ones, rest in peace.

Memorial to the Men
Who Died in World War II Secret Disaster

By John Fievet

At last, a long overdue tribute will be given to the 1,015 men who gave their lives in a war that was fought to protect our freedom. They died when the HMT Rohna was sunk by a guided missile launched from a German bomber on November 26, 1943 off the coast of North Africa. This was the greatest loss of American troops at sea in World War II. The Rohna, a vessel owned by the British-India Steam Navigation Company, was on charter to the British government and assigned to transport 1,982 American Troops to the China, Burma India theater. Only one day out of Oran, Algeria, the Rohna was steaming east through an area that had been identified as "Suicide Alley". The area got that name as a result of German success in inflicting heavy losses to Allied convoys using that route to India. When the War Department reported the loss of 1,015 men, they also acknowledged that over 800 bodies were never recovered. Only a family member can describe the anguish of never having remains to put to rest in the family plot. For them we hope that this memorial will bring some measure of peace.

This catastrophe was kept secret for decades. When the Rohna story was first brought to the attention of Charles Osgood with the CBS Radio Network on Veterans Day November 11, 1993, he verified the secrecy surrounding this event with the memorable words "It's not that we forgot, it's that we never knew". The same message was voiced recently by Mary Gadilhe, history teacher at John Carroll High School, when she wrote the following: The 50 Anniversaries of World War II are over but there is one anniversary that went unnoticed. On November 26, 1943,

1,015 United States service men lost their lives in the worst at-sea disaster of World War II. As a teacher of United States History for nineteen years, did I ever talk about this incident? No but no one else did either. And no one ever would have taught about it except for the efforts of a survivor of this secret tragic sinking in the Mediterranean". This brings up the question as to why the sinking of the Rohna was kept secret for decades after the war ended. Many have speculated that it was the fact that the death instrument for the Rohna was a missile still in its experimental stage. Of course, we have never seen an official document to validate that view. Others have expressed that it was the fact that our comrades met their fate on a British ship! The Rohna never became a household word as did the Arizona and the Indianapolis. We will never understand the position taken by the War Department when details of this tragedy were withheld from the families who lost loved ones on the Rohna. Mothers and fathers went to their graves never knowing how their sons met their fate. Some mothers, in desperation, went to fortune tellers in hopes that they could shed some light on their sons last hours on this earth. As late as August of 1993, a letter to the Pentagon requesting information on the event that took the life of her brother went unanswered. Who can justify this attitude? I'm sure that I speak for many survivors when I promise that we will continue to search for those who lost their loved ones to let them know the truth.

It is easy to understand why the British Government has so little information on the Rohna story in their archives. They certainly should be reluctant to let the relatives of the 1,015 men who died know that the Captain of the Rohna permitted their sons lives to be put in jeopardy by putting them on a ship with lifeboats that were hanging on chains rusted in place making it impossible to launch. Most of the rafts that were supposed to save lives went down with the ship permanently rusted to their slides. Also, no Captain would want it known that his crew was the first to leave the ship deserting the American troops and leaving them to launch the boats and rafts the best way that they could. One survivor reported that the Indian crew beat off with their oars troops that attempted to board their lifeboats. Is it any wonder that this information never made it into print!

I would like to conclude this eulogy with a verse I read some years ago. "Nothing beautiful in this world is ever lost. Those we cherish will live forever in our memory. A memory is a special treasure. Though times may pass, a memory stays; reminding us of happy days and of the people who have touched our lives. Of favors done and love expressed, of those who've stood above the rest. A memory is a treasure that survives."

Carl Schoenacker's Speech

At the Dedication of the Rohna Memorial Fort Mitchell, AL

May 30, 1996

Ms. Wright, Mr. William Trower, Mr. John Moore, members of the Memorial Day Committee, those on the podium, ladies and gentlemen.

I am glad that you are holding to the 30th. My hometown of Waterloo, N.Y. is too.

Some ten years ago our son took Ruth and I, and his young nephew, Adam, on an all day boat trip. We went through the locks from one of New York's Finger Lakes to another and back. We had a picnic lunch, some swimming. Adam was with his older cousin, Steven, and in his words it was awesome. At day's end, as we were about to step off the boat, Adam looked up at his Uncle Frank, "This is the best day of my life!".
I am not into superlatives as Adam is, but today is truly a great day, one I did not expect. I thank all of you for whatever you have done to make it possible, and more, I thank everyone, from the smallest donation and effort to the largest.
When we think of large efforts, we think of John Fievet. In 1951 when I was stonewalled by my senator, I did not know where to turn. John was stonewalled many times but kept turning and twisting. For 50 years I, and others, earned this like an undigested ball in my gut. John carried it in his head where his brains are. John never stopped. John was two decks below me on the Rohna but miles above me in this effort, and I,

and the entire group, am grateful to him, for the effort and I am grateful for allowing me to be a part of this.

From our first conversation it was obvious that John and I had a similarity of thought and word. We both reduced what we saw when we came topside on the Rohna to the same word, chaos. In my first speech I gave three goals. That evening I learned that these were John's goals as well.—Publicity, to make the public aware, a memorial to the 1015, and recognition for the crew of the Pioneer. Here we have unfinished business. They saved 600 of us and have not forgotten those they could not save.

I would like to mention Harrell Jones of the Pioneer. In 1943 he jumped into the Mediterranean to rescue men. In 1996 he found the Pioneer in Mexico.

John and I are also grateful to the wives, of the Pioneer crew, all wives. Ruth and Catherine have been great, and they are typical. These ladies traveled long distances, sat in long meetings, waited in hotel rooms, made new friends, and been supportive in every way possible. When they were not behind us they were out front leading us as Ruth was yesterday and Ruth Canney was through two reunions.

I have never been asked why I am so dedicated, but I have been reminded that I do not have to do this. In closing I will mention just two of the 1015 who died.

Sgt. William Reed, Bill Reed, was my buddy. It is surprising that we were not together when the ship was hit. I looked for him, I asked about him. I had confidence in him. I met each ship bringing in survivors. No one knew. When I read of a lost loved one, I now understand the feeling. Bill's wife has died. He has no family but I will not forget.

After one of my letters in a local paper I received a phone call from the sister of S/Sgt. Harvey Sanow, Mrs. Georgia Port of Newark, NY. Mrs.

Port thanked me and just wanted to talk as the family of victims often do. She told of how little they were told, of a memorial the family gave him, and that his wife had recently died, then she said that Harvey was married in July, 1943. That really hit home! Ruth and I were married the same week! When I was caught in undertow, I thought Ruth would never see me again, but somehow I got free. Harvey's wife never did see him again. It is this simple. I lived therefore I owe.

Perhaps I should be more like Adam. Perhaps it is awesome. Perhaps it is the best day of my life. Right now it seems that way. To all who made this day possible, I thank you very much.

How to Have a Marker Dedicated

By John Fievet

After helping Ruthann Hellemeyer and others remember their loved ones by dedicating a marker in their name, I realized that there is some information that might be useful to others in the group.

The first would be instructions for getting a marker. The Department of Veterans Affairs says that, "In national cemeteries, unrecovered remains can be memorialized individually or as a group. An individual memorial marker can be erected at government expense in a national cemetery when requested by a surviving next of kin. A group monument can be erected to memorialize all known and unknown dead who perished in a common military event and whose remains have not been recovered or identified." Just as I did for all lost on the Rohna and Ruthann did for her uncle, this is a tremendous way to leave a lasting memorial.

The second important information would be about requesting medals for next of kin lost in the war. My wife, Catherine has recently requested medals for her brother who died in France and I realized, again, that this could be helpful information to others. According to the information that I have, medals can be requested by completing Standard Form 180 or by a written request that includes a copy of the kin's discharge papers or notification of death/missing in action and sending it to the National Personnel Records Center (NPRC) at the following address:

National Personnel Records Center
9700 Page Avenue
St. Louis, MO 63132-5100

Once the initial request and papers are received the NPRC will look through the Veteran's military records to verify which medals he/she is eligible to receive. Medals will then be sent along with a form entitled, "Transmittal of and/or entitlement to awards."

I do hope others will look into either or both of these possibilities.

North Africa American Cemetery and Memorial

American Battle Monuments Commission

Location

North Africa American Cemetery and Memorial is situated 10 miles northeast of the city of Tunis, Tunisia, and 5 miles northeast of its airport (El Aouina). It may be reached by taxicab from the city or the airport. There is an electric commuter train from Tunis; the nearest stop is at Amilcar station, from which the cemetery is only two or three hundred yards distant. Hotels are available in Tunis, Carthage, Amilcar and Gammarth. The weather is likely to be quite hot during the summer months and cold on occasion during the winter.

Hours

The cemetery is open daily to the public from 9:00 am to 5:00 pm except December 25 and January 1. It is open on host country holidays. When the cemetery is open to the public, a staff member is on duty in the Visitors' Building to answer questions and escort relatives to grave and memorial sites.

History

Prior to entry into World War II, the United States adopted a strategic policy regarding how it would conduct combat operations should it be forced into war against the Axis powers (Germany and Italy) and Japan at the same time. The policy was to defeat the stronger enemy in Europe first, while simultaneously maintaining a vigorous defensive posture against Japan. It was not altered by the Japanese surprise attack at Pearl Harbor on 7 December 1941.

The basic plan of action advocated by U.S. war planners was to concentrate forces, supplies and materiel in the British Isles, and after a period of training, to launch a powerful amphibious across the English Channel in the summer of 1943. Although the German advance against Moscow had been stopped in December 1941 and the enemy had been forced backward by a strong Russian winter offensive, the Germans again began advancing rapidly in 1942. The Crimea was overrun, Sevastopol was captured and German forces were moving against Stalingrad on the Volga River. Even greater advances were being made in the Caucasus Mountains to the southeast.

Matters also were going badly for the British in the Mediterranean area along the coast of North Africa in Libya and Egypt, the area known as the Western Desert. There, where the fighting had been seesawing back and forth for nearly two years, the combined German-Italian force known as the Afrika Korps had forced the British Eighth Army back further into Egypt, and was closer to Alexandria than ever before. Additional Axis advances in Egypt and the Caucasus posed a threat to the entire Middle East.

The Allies sorely needed an offensive operation that would lessen the pressure on the British Eighth Army in Egypt. The only operation that could be undertaken with a reasonable chance of success was an assault in French Morocco and Algiers in northwest Africa. It had the advantage of getting American forces into action in 1942, although it would probably delay the cross-Channel assault planned for 1943. The Allies hoped that French forces defending northwest Africa, which were operating under the control of the portion of France which had not been occupied by the Germans after the armistice of 1940, might welcome them or offer only token resistance. Some of these forces were loyal to Vichy, France; others were sympathetic to the Allied cause. The invasion plan of northwest Africa provided for three naval task forces to land before dawn on 8 November 1942 in three widely separated areas. The U.S. Western Naval Task Force, composed entirely of American ships sailing from the United States at the height of the Battle of the Atlantic against German submarines, arrived unsuspected and undetected. Its landings in French Morocco encountered the strongest resistance of any of the landing forces. In the center, the U.S. 3rd Infantry Division landing at Fedala near Casablanca, found both army and naval forces opposing it. As it fought its way inland, fire from U.S. naval forces neutralized the shore batteries and sank several French warships. By 1500 hours, Fedala had fallen. The U.S. 3rd Division then closed on Casablanca where it met strong resistance, until on 11 November upon orders from Algiers, the French surrendered.

Further to the south, the 47th Regimental Combat Team of the U.S. 9th Infantry Division and the Combat Command B of the U.S. 2nd Armored Division established a bridgehead at Safi, against heavy ground and air resistance. When U.S. carrier planes joined the attack, Combat Command B drove northward toward Casablanca, halting only when it was informed that resistance had ceased. To the north, the 60th Regimental Combat Team of the U.S. 9th Division captured the Port Lyautey airfield late on 10 November, with the support of naval and armored units, When the British Center and Eastern Naval Task Forces coming from the United Kingdom passed through the Straits of Gibraltar, their presence was immediately reported to the enemy by spies. As the British Eighth Army had won a great victory at El Alamein just a few days before and now was pursuing the Afrika Korps westward toward Libya and Tunisia, the enemy assumed falsely that the task forces were en route to block the retreat of the Afrika Korps. Although the war and troop ships of the British Center Naval Task Force were British, the assault troops at Oran, as in French Morocco, were entirely American. Landing on both sides of the city, the U.S. 1st Infantry Division, elements of the U.S. 1st Amored Division and a battalion of Rangers met only sporadic resistance as they came ashore. Quickly, the infantry advanced toward the city while the armored units seized the airfields, where a U.S.

parachute battalion had previously been dropped nearby. The French capitulated at 1230 hours on 10 November.

The landing at Algiers from the ships of the British Eastern Naval Task Force encountered the least resistance. Debarking on both sides of the city, the force consisted of the U.S. 34th Infantry Division, the 39th Regimental Combat Team of the U.S. 9th Infantry Division, British Commandos and 3 elements of the British 78th Infantry Division. Opposition ended that same day, as orders from Algiers were issued to cease all hostilities in North Africa.

Meanwhile, the race for Tunisia had begun. Anticipating that the Allies next would move into Tunisia to seize the Tunis-Bizerte area, the enemy began moving troops as rapidly as possible into northern Tunisia by sea and air, even though fighting was still in progress at Oran and in French Morocco. The following day, the floating reserve of the British Eastern Naval Task Force, a brigade group of the British 78th Division, was dispatched eastward to the port of Bougie, in the first step of the Allied advance toward Tunisia. That evening, German and Italian forces moved into southern France as Italy prepared to seize Corsica.

At this stage of the war, it was clear to almost all Frenchmen that the future of France depended upon whether or not it joined with the Allies. Among the first to take this action was the French army commander in Tunisia. Although his forces were greatly outnumbered by the enemy, he slowly withdrew them into the mountains to establish contact with Allied troops moving eastward. As the number of troops on each side gradually strengthened, both the Allies and the Axis launched a series of attacks on Tunisia with indifferent success. By advent of the winter rains, it was clear that the British First Army and its attached French and American units were unable to oust the stronger German Fifth Panzer Army from Tunisia. A major factor was the enemy's superiority of air power.

In January 1943, the U.S. II Corps began arriving in southern Tunisia with some additional troops. At that time, the British First Army was organized from north to south into three corps; the British 5 Corps in the north, the French XIX Corps in the center, the U.S. II Corps in the south.

Throughout the next month and a half, the stronger enemy air and ground forces hammered away at the Allies in central and southern Tunisia. To reduce the effects of these attacks, U.S. units were dispersed throughout their area as were units of the French XIX Corps to the north.

Meanwhile, by early February the Afrika Korps had retreated across Libya and reached the Mareth Line, a series of old French fortifications in southern Tunisia. There it began to prepare a defense against the approaching British Eighth Army, whose pursuit had been slowed by major logistical problems.

Before the British Eighth Army arrived in strength, the German Fifth Panzer Army and the Afrika Korps launched a heavy armored assault against the widely-dispersed U.S. II Corps. In a series of sharp actions, the enemy forced a withdrawal, broke through the mountains near the Kasserine Pass into the valley beyond and achieved spectacular success. They were not halted until 22 February when combined American and British armored and infantry units and the U.S. 9th Division Artillery, which had been rushed to the scene from as far away as Oran, arrived in the nick of time to stem the assault.

Two more enemy attacks were repulsed, one in the north, the other against the British Eighth Army, of which only a few of its units had arrived. From that point onward, the initiative passed to the Allies. As the reorganized U.S. II Corps threatened the Mareth Line from the flank and rear, the British Eighth Army attacked frontally. Success was achieved when New Zealand and British troops outflanked the Afrika Korps' position and drove northward. During the same March period, the Allies gained control of the air. By mid-April, the enemy had been driven northward and was confined to a small area in northeast Tunisia consisting of Bizerte, Tunis and the Cape Bon Peninsula.

In preparation for the final Allied attacks, the U.S. II Corps was moved north opposite Bizerte. The British First Army's main effort was to be made in the center by the British 5 and 9 Corps, the latter corps having been organized when reinforcements were transferred from the British Eighth Army. On 19 April, the British Eighth Army began to attack in the south, but made little gain at great cost. Three days later the British First Army's main attack was launched and was met by a vigorous defense. In the center, very little progress was being made. However, the U.S. II Corps in the north and the French XIX Corps further south were making substantial gains.

At this time two additional divisions were transferred from the British Eight Army to strengthen the First Army's British 5 and 9 Corps. Utilizing the reinforcements, the attack resumed on 4 May, preceded by a devastating air bombardment. Little could be done to counter the bombardment as the enemy had withdrawn almost all its aircraft to Sicily. The U.S. II Corps captured Bizerte on 7 May and the British 5 and 9 Corps drove down to the Medjerda River to capture Tunis that same day. On 9 May, the enemy in the U.S. Corps area capitulated. By 13 May 1943, over one quarter of a million Axis troops had been taken prisoner.

The Site

The cemetery site covers 27 acres of the plateau lying between the Mediterranean and the Bay of Tunis, both of which are a mile or so distant. It is located near the site of the ancient Carthaginian city destroyed by the Romans in 146 B.C. and lies over part of the site of Roman Carthage. Some 200 yards to the east are remnants of Roman houses and streets — the entire region thereabouts contains vestiges of the Roman city as well as some remains of the Carthaginian era.

After the end of World War II survey made jointly by representatives of the Secretary of War and the American Battle Monuments Commission revealed that all of the sites of the temporary cemeteries established in North Africa during the war had major disadvantages. The present site was established in 1948. It lies in the sector of the British First Army which liberated the Tunis area in May 1943. Construction of the cemetery and memorial was completed in 1960.

Here rest 2,841 of our Military Dead, representing 39 percent of the burials which were originally made in North Africa and in Iran. A high proportion of these gave their lives in the landings in, and occupation of, Morocco and Algeria and in subsequent fighting which culminated in the liberation of Tunisia. Others died as a result of accident or sickness in these and other parts of North Africa, or while serving in the Persian Gulf Command in Iran.

Architects
Architects for the cemetery and memorial were Moore and Hutchins of New York City, New York. The landscape architect was Bryan J. Lynch also of New York.

General Layout
The main entrance from the eucalyptus-bordered highway is at the southeast corner of the cemetery. To the right of the entrance is one of the superintendent's houses; beyond is the oval forecourt. Beneath the green plot in the center of the forecourt is the reservoir which stores the water for the cemetery needs, as well as the pumps which operate the high pressure sprinkling system. All of the water comes from the municipal supply for which the storage area is located some miles to the south of the city of Tunis. Down the hill and beyond the forecourt is the utilities area.

In the forecourt are rows eucalyptus and ornamental India laurel fig (*Ficus nitida*) trees; the beds include Pittosporum tobira, scarlet hibiscus, Lantana camara, English ivy, Cassia floribunda, orangeberry pittosporum and other shrubs and vines. Extending to the left (west) of the forecourt and parking area is the mall. At the head of the steps leading to the mall, and at the right (north) is the Visitors' Building, built of Roman travertine marble imported from Italy; west it is the flagpole.

On the south side of the mall are the Tablets of the Missing; at its far (west) end is the memorial chapel. North of the mall is the graves area which it overlooks. South of the highway is an additional area used for services purposes.

The Tablets of the Missing

The Tablets of the Missing consist of a wall 364 feet long, of local Nahli limestone, with local Gathouna limestone copings. Built into it are panels of Trani limestone imported from Italy on which are inscribed the names and particulars of 3,724 of the Missing:

United States Army and Army Air Forces......................3,095

United States Navy..615

United States Coast Guard...14

These men gave their lives in the service of their Country; but their remains either were not identified or they were lost or buried at sea in the waters surrounding the African continent. They include men from all of the States except Hawaii and from the District of Columbia.

Without confirmed information, a War Department Administrative Review Board established the official date of death of those commemorated on the Tablets of Missing as one year and a day from the date on which the individual was in Missing in Action status.

At each end of the Tablets is this inscription:
*Here are recorded the names of Americans who gave their lives in the service of their country and who sleep in unknown graves 1941-45 * into thy hands o lord.*

Near the foot of the steps leading down from the forecourt is a pool and figure of honor about to bestow a laurel branch upon those who gave their lives. The figure's pedestal bears this inscription:
Honor to them that trod the path of honor.

Along the wall are two other sculptured figures: *Memory* and *Recollection*, the latter holding a book with the inscription *Pro Patria*. Between these figures are oak leaf wreaths within which are engraved the names of battles on land, sea and in the air, in which the American forces participated: Oran, Casablanca, Algiers, Kasserine, El Guettar, Sidi Nsir, Bizerte, Sicily, Ploesti. All of this sculpture is of Bianco Caldo stone from near Foggia, Italy; it was designed by Henry Kreis of Essex, Connecticut, and executed by Pietro Bibolotti, Pietrasanta, Italy.

Planted in front of the Tablets of the Missing are rows of India laurel fig trees *(Ficus nitida)* in beds of English ivy. On the north side of the terrace are rows of holly oaks *(Quercus ilex)* and potted pink geraniums adjacent to beds of ivy.

The Memorial
The memorial consists of the Court of Honor and the chapel. The Court of Honor is in the form of a cloister. Within it is a large rectangular stone of remembrance of black Diorite d'Anzola quarried in northwest Italy; this inscription, adapted from Ecclesiasticus XLIV, is worked into the design of the mosaic panel surrounding the base:
Some there be which have no sepulchre their name liveth for evermore.

The rectangular pylons of the cloister are of San Gottardo limestone from the vicinity of Vicenza in Italy; the main part of the structure of the memorial is faced with Roman travertine. The pavement is of Sienite della Balma granite from northwest Italy. In the southwest corner is a Russian oleve tree *(Elaeagnus angustifolia)*. On the west wall of the cloister facing the mall is this inscription, with translations in French and Arabic:
1941-1945
In proud remembrance of the achievements of her sons and in humble tribute to their sacrifices this memorial has been erected by the United States of America.

At the south end of the cloister are the maps. These are of ceramic, designed and fabricated by Paul D. Holleman of Roxbury, Massachusetts, from information supplied by the American Battle Monuments Commission.

The large map on the end (south) wall records the military operations of the American forces and those of the Allies in Morocco, Algeria and Tunisia from the initial "Torch" landing on 8 November 1942 to the Axis surrender on 13 May 1943. The descriptive text is in English, Arabic and French, of which this is the English version:

On 8 November 1942, in a major operation covered by naval gunfire and aircraft, United States and British troops were landed simultaneously in three widely separated areas on the shores of North Africa. The American western naval task force, sailing from the United States, landed American troops at Fedala, Mehdia and Safi for the assault on Casablanca. Other American units escorted from the United Kingdom by the British center naval task force went ashore near Oran and in two days occupied that city. Ships of the British eastern naval task force, coming also from the British Isles, landed United States and British troops near Algiers which was occupied that day. Following the landings, the allied naval forces kept the sea lanes open for an uninterrupted flow of supplies and also provided fire support to the troops ashore. On 11 November an armistice proclamation ended Vichy French resistance throughout Algeria and Morocco.

These allied forces then turned eastward toward Tunisia into which axis troops were steadily streaming. Moving rapidly, American and British units advanced across the frontier toward Tunis. Strong resistance, coupled with unfavorable weather and difficult supply conditions, checked this advance just 16 miles from its goal during the first week of December a counteroffensive in the Tebourba-Chouigui area pushed back the allied line between Jefna and Medjezx el Bab.

Immediately after the landings, allied air units had occupied existing North Africa bases and had aided the eastward advance, but lack of suitable for-

ward airfields and shortages of personnel and aircraft hampered their operations. During December and January axis forces, which had been strongly reinforced by sea and air, were aggressive in central and southern Tunisia. In mid-February they launched a pincers attack aimed at el kef which penetrated United States II corps position, pushed through a pass Northwest of Kasserine but was halted on 22 February before Thala.

One month later the British eight army turned the western flank of the Mareth line and drove the enemy northward to Enfidaville. The French xix corps held fast in its mountain positions near Maktar. By March 1943 the allies had gained control of the skies over Africa. The final campaign opened in northwest Tunisia on 22 April 1943. The United States II corps, now on the allied left flank, pushed eastward, reducing successive defensive positions in difficult hilly terrain, liberating Mateur, Ferryville and Bizerte. Meanwhile the British 5 and 9 corps were engaged in a determined assault down the Medjerda river which culminated in freeing the city of Tunis. In the ii corps area the enemy capitulated on 9 may. By 13 may, denied escape by allied mastery of the sea and air, one quarter of a million axis troops then remaining in Tunisia became prisoners of war.

On this wall also are the two series of key maps — "The War against Germany" and "The War against Japan."

As indicated by the texts, the map on the east wall records in greater detail the operations in central and southern Tunisia, while the one on the opposite (west) wall covers the final stages in northern Tunisia.

The map on the west pylon portrays most of Africa, the Mediterranean and the Middle East. It records the air ferry routes across Africa as well as the operations of the Persian Gulf Command. The descriptive text for this map, also in English, French and Arabic, is on the face of the corresponding east pylon. The English text follows:

The United States of America, while contributing its land, sea, and air forces to the prosecution of World War II, also aided its many allies by fur-

nishing military equipment and supplies. Items of all kinds were carried by vast fleets of steamships to every available port. In this effort also aircraft were ferried from the United States across the Atlantic Ocean and central Africa to Cairo, Karachi and Basra. Through the Persian gulf command area, the United States delivered, from 1942 to 1945, nearly 4 1/2 million tons of supplies to the U.S.S.R. these included 4,874 aircraft of which 995 were flown in; over 160,000 tanks, armored cars and trucks, 140,000 tons of guns, ammunition and explosives; 550,000 tons of petroleum products; 950,000 tons of food; and 1,000,000 tons of metal and metal products. The United States also furnished to the U.S.S.R. through other ports, more than 13 million tons of additional supplies.

The Chapel

The bronze doors and the windows of the chapel were fabricated by the Morris Singer Company of London, England. At the far end of the chapel, which is lighted by the tall window on the right and a row of lower windows on the left is the altar of white Carrara marble, with this inscription from St. John X:28: *I give unto them eternal life and they shall never perish* ***

The wall behind the altar is of polished Rosso Porfirico marble from near Udine in northeastern Italy. Facing the door, on the wing wall projecting from the right, is the sculpture *Sacrifice* carved in Italian Bianco Caldo stone, designed by Henry Kreis and executed by Pietro Bibolotti. Below and to its left is this inscription from Shelley's ode "Adonais": *"He has outsoared the shadow of our night."*

To the left of the altar are the United States national flag and Christian and Jewish chapel flags. Projecting from the east wall above the pews are the flags of combat arms, viz. Infantry, Field Artillery, Navy Infantry Battalion, Air Corps and Armor. Beneath the flags is this prayer: *Almighty god, receive these thy heroic servants into thy kingdom.*

The ceiling is of Moroccan cedar; the pews and prie-dieu are of walnut. Three flower boxes of teakwood, with bronze appurtenances, are located under the west windows of the chapel. North of the chapel, down a flight of steps from the cloister, is the memorial garden with its pool; the plants include latana, poinciana, pink geraniums and a Jerusalem thorn tree *(Parkinsonia aculeate)*. Beyond is the graves area.

The Graves Area

The 2,833 headstones in the rectangular graves area are divided into nine plots designated A to I. They are arranged in rectangular lines harmonizing with the rectangular composition of the cemetery and memorial. The 2,841 burials in the cemetery include 240 Unknowns. These Dead who gave their lives in their Country's service came from all of the States except Hawaii and from the District of Columbia; a few came from foreign countries. Among the headstones is one which marks the tomb of seven Americans whose identity is unknown; also two adjacent headstones mark the graves of four men whose names are known but whose remains could not be separately identified; a bronze tablet between these graves records their names. Also in this cemetery, in three instances, two brothers are buried side by side.

In the burial area are four fountains and pools of Roman travertine, which with their surrounding vegetation of rosemary, oleander, and pink geraniums form small and welcome oases in this frequently hot climate. The paths are lined either by India laurel fig *(Ficus nitida)* or California pepper trees *(Schinus molle)*. The border massifs contain a wide variety of trees and shrubs in which oleanders and hibiscus are predominant.

Visitors' Building

On the west facade of the Visitors' Building is this inscription taken from General Eisenhower's dedication of the Golden Book now enshrined in St. Paul's Cathedral in London:
Here we and all who shall hereafter live in freedom will be reminded that to these men and their comrades we owe a debt to be paid with grateful

remembrance of their sacrifice and with the high resolve that the cause for which they died shall live.

Within the Visitors' Building is a Roman mosaic discovered in the region and donated in 1959 by President Bourhguiba of Tunisia to Ambassador G. Lewis Jones, who in turn presented it to the cemetery.

Plantings

The grass in the cemetery is kikuyu *(Pennisetum clandestinum)*. It can sustain the heat of this region with minimum water. The entire graves and memorial areas are surrounded beyond the inner walls by massifs of trees and shrubbery in which these predominate: pyramidal cypress *(C. pyramidalis)*, aleppo pine *(P. halepensis)*, eucalyptus *(E. gomocephala)*, cassowary *(Casuarina tenuissima)*, Moreton Bay fig *(Ficus macrophilla)*, goldenwattle acacia *(Acacia pycnantha)*, as well as weaver's broom *(Spartium junceum)* and some 3,000 oleanders.

List of Casualties

- A -

Adam, Richard J., Cpl., 36317587, AC
Adamczyk, Jacob E., T/5, 36721878, CE
Aguilar, Gilbert, Pfc., 18198769, SC
Albrecht, Paul E., T/4, 38027398, MC
Alexander, Walter J., T/5, 34315650, MC
Alfred, Edward H., Pfc., 36448909, AC
Alleman, Roger E., Pfc, 35496862, CE
Allen, Ramon R., Sgt., 39906599, CE
Allen, Steve, T/5, 35682721, CE
Amarello, John J., Pfc, 32577653, AC
Anctil, Ronaldo J., T/5, 31218820, CE
Anger, Earl J., 2 Lt, 01107548, CE
Antrasian, Thomas, Pfc., 12183162, SC
Archer, Perry O., Pvt., 39385085, SC
Arnold, Alfred N., Pvt., 37495985, CE
Arnold, Kenneth L., Pvt., 35541018, CE
Arvickson, Oscar R., Pvt., 33570089, CE
Ashford, Harry B., T/5, 37180070, CE
Ashworth, Elmer, Pfc, 38425097, CE
Atkinson, Jackson P., T/4, 34306534, SC
Attanasi, Americo J., Cpl., 33477038, AC

- B -

Baack, Walter W., Pvt., 38370636, CE
Babin, Edward J., Lt., 0-650198
Bacco, Daniel A., Pfc., 32792671, CE
Baine, John W., Pvt, 33363224, AC
Baker, Harry F., Pvt., 35541070, CE
Baker, Richard W., Pvt., 31253360, CE
Ballerino, Frank, Pvt., 32367983, SC
Banks, George L., Pvt., 33494107, SC
Bannon, Dwight F., Sgt., 19100125, INF.
Barbala, John, Pvt., 33460241,

Barrett, Elmer, Cpll., 19059298, AC
Barthel, William G., S/Sgt, 32461142, CE
Bartko, Walter, Pvt., 33423068, CE
Basile, Giacomo D., Pvt., 33592062, SC
Battista, Nunzio, T/5, 32539505, SC
Beatty, Cletus E., Sgt., 39614465, CE
Beck, Louis H., Cpl., 33287444, AC
Beckham, Sam D., Pvt., 38451361, CE
Behn, Otto J., Sgt., 37085417, INF.
Bellavia, Ettore, Pvt., 12043025, SC
Belles, Kermit A., Pvt., 39208000, AC
Benderling, Frank L., T/5, 36293611, CE
Bennafield, William F., Pvt., 34058562, CE
Bennett, Robert O., Pfc., 12182941, SC
Berger, Leon, Sgt., 32185961, AC
Berns, Edward J., T/5, 37409403, CE
Bernstein, Joseph, S/Sgt., 31201781, CE
Berry, James J., T/4, 32568479, SC
Bessonette, John I., T/5, 34611701, CE
Beyer, Clarence W., T/5, 36291312, CE
Bielski, Joseph E., Pvt., 31352919, AC
Biggs, Otis L., T/5, 38363231, CE
Bird, Leo J., T/Sgt, 32312785, SC
Birkel, Jack T., Pfc., 18133235, AC
Bishop, Herman C., Pfc., 32668261, CE
Blackman, Howard M., Pvt., 34809002, CE
Blaine, Franklin W., Sgt, 38000292, INF.
Blake, George G., Cpl., 33450376, INF.
Blake, William F., Pfc., 35528208, CE
Bloom, Robert L., Pvt., 33465212, SC
Bobby, John, Pfc., 32539552, SC
Bogovich, Stephan M., T/5, 36599215, CE
Bohnet, Livingston R., Pfc., 19185345, AC
Bolyard, Raymond V., Sgt., 15323725, CE
Bonacci, August P., Cpl, 32675485, CE

Boos, Raymond W., Pvt., 36297827, CE
Boroch, Theodore T., Cpl., 37124298, AC
Bouchard, George A., T/5, 31084293, MC
Bowden, Milford N (?), Pfc, 33569338, CE
Boyd, Benjamin F., Cpl., 17127236, AC
Boyer, James C., Sgt., 20462441, INF
Branam, James F., T/5, 34504709, CE
Brandon, William L., Pvt., 39905493, CE
Bresee, Theodore F. Jr., Cpl., 12171543, AC
Brewster, Carl W., Pvt., 33436359, CE
Brezinskey, John F., S/Sgt., 13022884, AC
Bricker, Harold L., Pfc., 33496858, CE
Broner, Max, T/5, 39563201, CE
Brooks, Paul M., S/Sgt., 34206526, AC
Brown, Eugene J., Pfc., 35602619, CE
Brown, Lelland Bb., T/5, 35746768, CE
Brown, Walter L., Pfc., 35539837, CE
Brumbaugh, Jack C., Cpl., 14177846, AC
Bruner, Landen, Sgt., 34597179, CE
Bruno, Orlando S., Pfc, 39906691, AC
Bryant, Clifford D., Cpl., 37108597, AC
Bryce, Neuman H., Sgt., 38300275, AC
Buchanan, Earl O., Cpl., 39270712, AC
Buchanan, Russel G., Pfc., 33288164, CE
Buckingham, Millard E., T/4, 32367947, SC
Bucy, Weldon E., Pfc., 37410176, CE
Buie, Richard E., Cpl., 18167012, CE
Buis, Charles W., Cpl., 35563638, AC
Bullard, Orison J., Jr., T/5, 36555663, CE
Burazio, Patsy, Pfc., 35602632, CE
Burk, Charles E., Pvt., 36450603, CM
Burke, Manuel T., T/5, 33531378, CE
Burke, William J., Pvt., 32775397, SC
Burnett, Glenn F., Sgt., 36417867, CE
Butler, Edward T., Cpl., 32668390, CE
Butler, Frank S., Cpl., 14139084, AC
Byrne, John A., T/5, 36721723, CE

- C -

Caldwell, Paul B., Pfc., 34597054, CE
Calli, John J., Pvt., 32865348, CE
Calvert, Julius C., Pfc., 35646093, CE
Cambridge, Donald, Cpl., 39194428, AC
Cameron, John C., Cpl., 17155716, AC
Campbell, James P., Pvt., 35599176, CE
Campbell, John C., Cpl., 14184597, AC
Campbell, William J., Pvt., 37496932, CE
Caperton, William R., Pfc., 34713733, AC
Carel, Clarence E., Cpl., 35623839, CE
Carey, William G., Pfc., 18166240, CE
Carlin, Sanford R., Sgt., 12045147, AC
Carlson, Nils G., T/4, 33478545, CE
Carr, Michael, T/5, 32368012, SC
Carr, Thomas V., Cpl., 34388525, AC
Carrera, Henry A., Cpl., 18013973, CE
Casey, Earl S., Cpl., 13153 638, AC
Casey, Thomas M. Pfc., Ce, 32579812, CE
Casilio, William A., Pvt., 33668088?, CE
Castaneda, Henry L., Pfc, 39250907, NC
Caston, Cleo T., T/5, 37104251, CE
Catanzaro, Anthony, Pfc, 32693339,
Cattalini, Armand J., Pvt., 39036909, CE
Cebulski, Michael J., Pvt., 32878444, CE
Celmer, Stanislaus Jr., Sgt., 12029464, AC
Cenami, Frank P., Pvt., 31173205, AC
Chaney, Charles E., Pfc., 33577056, CE
Chapman, John H., T/5, 33412534, CE
Chavez, Frank M., T/5, 39276527, CE
Chavez, Salvador A., Cpl., 36653054, AC
Christopher, John A., Pfc., 32549972, CE
Clark, Leland A., Cpl., 36653054, AC
Clegg, George L., Cpl., 35488526, AC
Cline, Hal J., Pvt., 34595942, CE
Close, George M., Pfc., 39906648?, CE
Cochran, Charlie E., Pfc, 36393637, CE
Cochran, Howard B., S/Sgt., 14030216, AC
Coffee, Grover B., Pvt., 38327052, CE
Cohen, Sidney, Pvt., 32539852, SC

Cole, Otis Q., Pvt., 34596025, CE
Coleman, George E., T/5, 32736557, CE
Coleman, Richard H., Pvt., 36295201, CE
Coles, Saint M., Pfc., 6284733, AC
Collins, Livingston N., Pfc., 38380395, CE
Collins, William A., Pvt., 34811027, CE
Colon, Joseph A., Pfc., 32800729, AC
Comeaux, Dallas L., Pvt., 34236348, SC
Comer, Frederick W., Pvt., 32568300, SC
Conklin, Lester Jr., T/4, 32726038, CE
Conner, Earl V., Pvt, 13117014, AC
Conner, Harold R., Cpl., 31226126, AC
Conners, John F., Pvt., 31101569, AC
Conrad, James B., Cpl., 13142958, AC
Conrad, Joseph W., T/4/, 12165546, SC
Conroy, Joseph T., T/5, 32569893, SC
Conti, Sam S., Pvt., 36630857, CE
Cook, Forrest A., Sgt., 34506081, CE
Cooke, Edgar V., Pvt., 34597028, CE
Corcoran, Lawrence B., T/5/, 33331810, CE
Correa, Calvin R., Pvt., 36483076, AC
Coss, Earl R., Cpl., 39192681, AC
Cox, John T. Jr., Pfc., 31280802, CE
Coyle, William E., Cpl., 35661579,
Craig, John F., Pvt., 35602681, CE
Craig, Joseph W., Pvt.], 35647413, CE
Cranford, Douglas N., T/5, 34597271, CE
Creighton, Arthur J., Pfc., 11115307, AC
Cremer, Clarence E. Jr., Pvt., 35537363, SC
Cresse, Russel D., Pfc., 35613424, AC
Crum, Clinton W., T/5, 34610764, CE
Currey, Thomas, Pfc., 38306081, CE
Cusack, Joseph J., Pfc., 32568288, SC
Czernak, Edward J., Pfc., 36631962, CE

- D -

Dahm, Edmund A., Sgt., 36648807, AC
Dalton, Archie A., Pvt., 34505173, CE
Dandrea, Frank, Sgt., 33194784, CE

Danese, Angelo P, Pfc., 32569440, SC
Daniel, Paul L., Pvt., 37495201, CE
Daniel, Thomas S., S/Sgt., 14138168, AC
Daniels, Fletcher H., T/Sgt., 39200364, CE
Davis, Cecil J. Jr., T/5, 35682949, CE
Dawson, Clarence J., Cpl., 32412866, AC
Dawson, Paul, Pvt., 35742383, SC
Day, Elmer F., Sgt., 32487149, CE
De Mello, Alfred J., Pvt., 39123031, CE
Dean, Clarence, T/5, 38306563, CE
Dean, Frazier A., T/5, 38450863, CE
Deareuff Deardeoff, Melvon S., Pvt.,
   37505711, CE
Dearing, Henry M., T/5, 35599139, CE
Debonis, Joseph L., Jr., Pvt., 32569906, SC
Degennaro, Louis J., T/5, 32539554, SC
Dehart, Ransom A., T/5, 34596079, CE
Delameter, Jr., Roland M.., T/5, 39262653, AC
Delano, Jr., Roland M., Cpl., 11034336, AC
Deletto, William S., Cpl., 32503321, AC
Dell, William S., Sgt., 33496897, CE
Dellaflora, Anthony, Cpl., 35614206, AC
Delorenzo, Mario L., T/5, 12183359, SC
Deluca, Fred J., Pvt., 32911773, CE
Deodati, Ralph, T/4/, 32692157, CE
Deutsch, Leonard, Cpl., 12159691, AC
Devore, Forest L., Pfc., 35527668, CE
Dhom, Robert J., Pfc., 36633830, CE
Di Benedetto, Joseph, Pfc., 32742460, CE
Dickson, Albert J., Cpl., 37222195, AC
Dingman, Ernest, Pfc., 35683168, CE
Dingman, Jack C., Pvt., 37411323, CE
Dinittes, Peter J., Cpl., 13110516,
Dinnini, Arnold, Pfc., 33496919, CE
Dirsa, James, Jr, Cpl., 31110226,
Disbrow, Thomas C., Cpl., 32489262, AC
Doak, Joseph L., Cpl., 33338476, AC
Dobbins, George B., Sgt., 33360376, AC
Dockmam, Clarence B., Pfc., 36568363, CE
Doenges, Clarence J., Pvt., 33418940?, CE

Donahue, Harold P., Pfc., 12181832, SC
Donahue, John E., Pvt., 38380490, CE
Doyle, Raymond E., Sgt., 33310568, AC
Doyle, William A., Sgt., 15041604, AC
Du Vall, Claude E., Pfc., 35096207, CE
Dudley, Loyd T., Pvt., 33521051, CE
Duke, Lee F., Pvt., 38394647, CE
Dunbar, Donald W., Cpl., 33577308, AC
Duran, Leo H.., Pvt., 39551354, CE
Duren, Raymond O., Cpl., 14174678, AC
Durham, Harold W., T/5, 35536311, CE
Durham, Lucien N., T/5, 34526413, CE
Durkin, John J., Cpl., 32550629, AC
Dyda, Frank W., T/4, 32568284, SC

- E -

Eagle, Oscar F., T/5, 35682444, CE
Eastlack, William T., T/4, 32367920, SC
Eatmon, John G., Pvt., 39460356, CE
Ebling, William H., 2 Lt., 0-739411, AC
Economy, Charles J., T/5, 17107505,
Efstia (Efstis), John M., Pfc., 32604812, AC
Eidem, Ervin C., Cpl., 37320954, AC
Ekiss, Richard L., 1st Sgt., 6828735, AC
Ellington, Albert, T/5, 34723815, CE
Elliott, Lee, Sgt., 38394634, CE
Ellis, Donald B., T/4, 12133695, SC
Englert, Francis L., T/5, 37494782, CE
Enright, Walter T., Pfc., 32835971, AC
Ensminger, Freddie, Pvt., 38450974, CE
Epstein, Julius L., 1 Lt., 0-530241, CE
Espitia, Bernadino S., Pfc., 38340227, CE
Estes, Raymond C., Cpl., 19180159, AC
Eubanks, John M., Pvt., 35676992, AC
Evans, Raymond E, Pvt., 35676992, AC

- F -

Faber, Donald E., Pvt., 16131979, AC
Fairhurst, William M., Pvt, 33333920, SC

Falconer, John E. Jr., Pfc, 39274120, AC
Fallon, John J. Jr., Pvt., 12156727, AC
Farrel, Marion J., 1 Lt., 0669228, AC
Farrell, Robert E., Cpl., 39847477, MC
Farrow, James D., Pfc., 19033249, AC
Faulkner, William H., T/4, 34613764, CE
Favaro, Valentine S., Pfc., 36630811, CE
Feldman, Hyman, Pvt., 32792941, CE
Feldman, Sydney H., Pfc, 37603341, AC
Ferguson, Claude S, Pvt., 33647985, AC
Ferschweiler, Albert J., S/Sgt, 37284534, SC
Fesce, James, Pvt., 32914981, AC
Fields, Kenneth G., Pvt., 33423004, CE
Figuaroa, Alfredo M., T/5, 39854535, CE
Filburn, Robert G., Pfc., 35629804, MC
Fine, Lewis M., Sgt., 39460359, CE
Finn, Edward D., Pvt., 35541037, CE
Finn, William J., Pfc., 12211677, AC
Firsich, Francis L., Pfc., 35698788, AC
Fischetti, Pasquale R., Pvt., 32611060, CE
Fishell, Elmer H., T/5, 33208576, CE
Fisk, Willis R., Pvt., 32548865, CE
Fitzpatrick, Paul J., S/Sgt., 34205120
Flatt, Karl R. (Earl), Pvt., 34526780, CE
Flores, Robert P., Cpl., 18218754, AC
Flynn, Thomas K., T/5, 35683294, CE
Fondoble, Kenneth S., Pfc., 37499616, CE
Fong, Lou B., Pfc., 39036014, CE
Fontaine, Norman G., Pfc., 31247371, CE
Fontenot, Murphy A., Pfc., 38266112, CE
Foraker, Herbert G., Pfc., 35599281, CE
Ford, Douward, T/5, 37602711, CE
Forhan, Phillip A., 2 Lt, 0-580731, AC
Fortine (Fortin), Walter E., Cpl., 11122257, AC
Foster, James E., Pvt., 34326766, SC
Foster, William H., M/Sgt., 6731342
Fowler, Robert O., Pvt., 35510502, CE
Francisco, Joseph M., Pvt., 31136422, SC
Freeman, John W., Cpl., 35599306, CE

Freidenreich, Harry, Cpl., 32784433, AC
Friend, Alvin T., Pfc., 32465425, AC
Fuhrmark, Arhur E., Pfc., 35577180, AC
Fumic, Michael P., T/5, 35521541, CE
Funk, James P., Pfc., 32539654, SC
Fura, Richard, T/5, 32288793, SC
Fusco, Daniel L., Cpl., 33572338, AC

- G -

Gaborski, George, T/5, 12137107, CE
Gallegos, John J., Pfc., 39906711, CE
Gallo, Antonio, Pfc., 31277801, CE
Galvin, Mervin, Cpl., 35589254, AC
Garafalo, Charles, Pvt., 32651534, AC
Garcia, Feliciano, Pvt., 38425348, CE
Garcia, Rogelio, Pvt., 38364139, CE
Garza, Margarito, Pvt, 37472268, CE
Gates, Donald L., Pfc 37472268, CE
Gatto, Ludovico J., Pfc., 11114748, AC
Geher, Georgew., Cpl., 32206340, AC
Genovese, Joseph, Pfc., 32539446, SC
Gerity, Richard V., T/5, 32163016, SC
Gibbs, Horace J., Pvt., 34606529, CE
Giglio, Daniel F., T/4, 12183313, SC
Gilbert, Harry A., Cpl., 12048994, AC
Gillert, Henry E., T/4, 38306671, CE
Gillespie, Norman J., Pfc., 38326472, CE
Gipson, Leonard H., Cpl., 18098111, AC
Gluck, Bert M., Pfc., 12124131, AC
Glussek, John A., Pvt., 32731086, CE
Goldberg, Morris, T/5, 32568289, SC
Golecki, Edward J., Pfc., 33458918, AC
Gomes, Harold, T/Sgt, 6691285, AC
Goodman, Eugene R., Pvt., 19106356, AC
Goodwin, Alvin C., T/Sgt, 14091027, SC
Goracy, Marion F., Pvt., 32606776, SC
Gorman, Andrew, T/5, 39615313, CE
Gossman, Hyman, Pfc., 32786675, CE
Grace, Robert P., Sgt., 13030595, AC

Gracely, John M., T/5, 33230225, SC
Graham, Roderick M., T/5, 32732589, CE
Gray, John L., Pfc., 32182910, CE
Green, Theodore E., T/3, 6910869, CE
Greenlee, Leonard, S/Sgt., 39851826, SC
Greer, Ernest B., Sgt., 31178444, AC
Griffen, Earl K., Pfc., 32859799, AC
Griffin, Jesse E., T/5, 34505593, CE
Griffin, Martin J., Cpl., 32679301, CE
Griffith, Herman C., Pvt., 34505593, CE
Grimes, W.D., T/5, 18186752, CE
Grimstad, Gordon A., T/3, 36049805, MC
Grzywacz, Henry, Pvt., 32582241, SC
Guarneri, Charles, Sgt., 32692235, AC
Guastella, James V., Cpl., 32693526, AC
Guidry, Dennis, Pvt., 38483122, CE
Gunn, Abraham, Pvt., 32698154, CE
Gunther, King P., Cpl., 36115698
Gust, Carlos P., 1 Lt., 0-578999, AC
Gutierrez, Raymond J., T/4, 38349829, CE
Gyer, Joe R., Pvt., 37602853, CE

- H -

Habib (Habir), Rudolph, Pfc., 12188406, AC
Hackett, Jack D., Pvt., 33601802, AC
Haedel, John L., T/Sgt, 33027266, AC
Hale, Calvin H., T/5, 34506102, CE
Hale, Charlie B., Pvt., 39280034, CE
Haley, Percy E., Cap't, 0-499087, CE
Hall, Dalma B., Sgt., 34361906, CE
Hall, Joseph C., T/5, 38446231, CE
Hall, Noel, T/5, 37495376, CE
Hamilton, Harold R., T/5, 35683606, CE
Hamilton, James, Pvt., 35430362, CE
Hammond, Malcolm H., Pfc., 34399556, SC
Hankins, Ronald J., Sgt., 39267801, CE
Hann, Earle V., Sgt., 20347514, AC
Hanners, Grover, Pvt., 35657925, AC
Hansard, James F., Sgt., 39303420, AC

Hansen, John F., Sgt., 37397807, CE
Hanson, Merlin D., Pvt., 17155370, CE
Harmon, Clarence R., Cpl., 35602693, CE
Harmon, Clause A., Pvt, 36568200, CE
Harner, William C., Sgt., 14142014, AC
Harney, Joseph F. Jr., Pfc, 35562423, AC
Harrell, Clarence W., Pfc., 33522642, CE
Harrington, Charles J., Pfc., 36416502, CE
Harrison, Jarius, Sgt., 33283416, AC
Hartzell, James E, Pfc., 35710754, AC
Hatch, Byron G., Cpl., 18153995, AC
Hawkins, Andrew J., T/5, 34504593, CE
Hayden, Paul E., Sgt., 32364212, AC
Hayes, Peter E., Pvt., 31299692, CE
Hefferman, Robert M., Pfc., 32696901, AC
Heironymus, Wallace R., Cpl., 37468758, CE
Heller, Lawrence, Cpl., 36742014, CE
Henning, Marion W., T/5, 36416484, CE
Herd, Marlyn C., T/5, 37248017, MC
Herkel, Robert W., T/5, 36416484, CE
Herman, Walter P., Sgt., 34597593, AC
Herrmann, Doyle M., Pfc., 38394568, CE
Hester, Lester C., Pvt., 38267210, CE
Hewett., William H., Cpl., 12165712, AC
Hiatt, Robert C., Sgt, 38016092, CE
Hicks, Jackson C. Jr., Cpl., 18190306, cE
Hicks (Hichs), Walter C., Pfc, 34730907, AC
Hiler, Bayard D., Cpl., 33244510, AC
Hill, Earl I, Pvt., 38445205, CE
Hill, James T., Pfc., 38422775, CE
Hill, John B., Cpl., 36647110, AC
Hinds, Casper W., Cpl., 34494079, CE
Hinton, Herschel V., Cpl., 35614264, AC
Hischke, Frank, D. P., T/Sgt., 35551558
Hively, Harvey W., Pfc, 36447253, CE
Hoak, Donald E., Pvt., 33422998, CE
Hobbs, John E., Sgt., 19163121, AC
Hoehns, Joe, Pvt., 33524336, AC
Hogan, Carlton P., Cap't, 0-1688092, AC
Holland, Charles A., Pfc., 34442495, MC

Holloway, Archie C., Cpl., 13135505, AC
Holloway, Robert S., T/5/, 35648025,
Hook, Andrew J. Jr., 1 Lt., 0-577965, AC
Hooks, Jack M., 1 Lt., 0-1107439, CE
Hooper, Roy, T/5, 38473056, CE
Hopkins, Walter E., Pvt., 36416691, CE
Horton, George W., Pvt., 37397555, CE
Hostetler, Robert W., T/5, 35599226, CE
Hott, Raymond L., Pvt., 39907523, CE
Hoyle, William R., Pvt., 39907523, CE
Huffman, Elmer L., Pvt., 38429386, AC
Humka, Joseph S., Pvt., 33582809, CE
Humphries, William D., Pvt., 34724198, AC
Hunt, William H., Pvt., 33569374, CE
Hunter, Harry B., Pfc., 35455056, AC
Hutchins, Gilmer B., Pvt., 36612845, CE
Hutton, David, Pvt., 35532040, CE
Hynds, Hugh B., Pvt., 31241244, CE

- I -

Isaacson, Frank, Pvt, 32876511, INF.

- J -

Jackson, Robert F., Pvt., 38207374, AC
Jackson, Victor E., Pfc., 36440667, AC
Jacobs, Roy A., M/Sgt., 13065519, SC
Jacoby, Edward, Sgt., 20723161, INF.
Jaggers, Clarence T., Pvt., 32487119, CE
Janesick, Frank, Sgt., 36510522, AC
Janiszewski, Frank J., Pfc., 33370996, AC
Jarbala, John, Pvt., 33460241, CE
Jauernick, Edmund V., Cpl., 13110411, AC
Jeleniewski, Vincent T., T/4, 12165531, SC
Jenkins, Howard W., Pfc., 35641363, AC
Jenkins, Jacob K., Pvt, 32487176, CE
Jenkins, Tildon D., Sgt., 6928655, AC
Jerram, Charles K., T/5, 12183435, AC
Jessip, Chester W., Cpl., 20724350, INF.
Jesup, Fred I., Pfc., 35143059, SC

Jeter, Harold L., Pfc., 38473040, CE
Johansonn, Carl E., Sgt., 6978675, INF.
Johnson, Bufurd E., Cpl., 38427614, CE
Johnson, Carl W., Pvt., 36182326, AC
Johnson, Clarence C., Pfc., 18122537, AC
Johnson, Donald I., T/4, 36617774, CE
Johnson, Frank A., Pfc., 39906712, CE
Johnson, Grover C. Jr., Pvt., 33423107, CE
Johnson, John C., Pfc., 39195422, AC
Johnson, Joseph H., Pfc., 32386004, SC
Johnson, Leonard R., Pfc., 37493476, AC
Johnson, Marion O., Pvt., 35128700, SC
Jokel, James H., S/Sgt, 15329937, AC
Jolly, Jordan H., Pvt., 34526696, CE
Jones, Edward B., Cpl., 34508538, AC
Jones, Elmer L., T/4, 39036103, CE
Jones, Eugene N. (homes), T/Sgt., 32080515,
  AC
Jones, Homer S., Pvt., 38445243, CE
Jones, Roy, Pfc., 35625759, AC
Jones, Strother M., Pfc., 35683631, CE
Joseph, Frankin R., Sgt., 33167369, AC
Julian, Leonard L., Pvt., 37221505, SC

- K -

Kalamaras, George G., Sgt., 36724082, CE
Kaluba, Albert A., Pvt., 36647203, CE
Kamper, Martin B., Cpl., 37034977, INF
Karas, George J., Pfc., 35528146, CE
Karsten, William R., Pvt., 36724063, CE
Katt, Charles W., Sgt., 32596914, INF.
Kay, Lawrence L., 2 Lt, 0-650536, AC
Kearns, Henry, Pfc., 36613155, CE
Keating, William E., Cpl, 35682144, CE
Kefron, Earl W., Cpl., 35512550,?
Keiper, William L., T/5, 33569364, CE
Kelly, Edward R. Jr., Sgt., 32450631, AC
Kelly, James P., Pvt., 32720224, CE
Kemp, James H., Cpl., 14018829, AC

Kessler, Joseph A., Pvt., 35679723, CE
Kielbania, Mitchell C., Sgt., 31007306, INF
Kiernan, Bernard J., Pfc., 32594055, MC
Kiffney, Edward J., Pfc., 12172031, SC
King, Earl W., Cpl., 35493088, AC
King, George, Pvt., 34505507, CE
King, John P., Pvt., 38425101, CE
King, Paul S., S/Sgt, 34303760, SC
Kirk, Sidney H., Pvt., 33570085, CE
Kirkland, Carl, M/Sgt., 6348697, AC
Kirkpatrick, Raymond Jr., Pfc., 37493525, AC
Kitch, Harry L., 2 Lt, 0-1107521, CE
Klehm, Elsworth C., Pfc., 32609100,
Klein, Vancel A., Pvt., 38433270, AC
Klopf, Howard G., Pfc., 36558680, CE
Knowles, James W., Pfc., 36440529, CE
Kocur, Henry L., Cpl., 32535960, AC
Kofron, Robert J., Cpl., 35512550, AC
Kolobus, Benjamin W., T/5, 12172068, SC
Kordecki, Frank S., Pvt., 33422633, CE
Koscianski, Stephan V., T/5, 32368010, SC
Koski, Everett K., Pvt., 31262132, CE
Kramer, Bernard M., Pvt, 35540194, CE
Krapp, Arnold R., Pfc., 36440830, CE
Kraus, Robert H., Pvt., 33412073, INF.
Krisher, Walter E., Cpl., 35373418, AC
Krumwiede, Earl W., Pfc., 32734590,]AC
Kruse, John F., Pvt., 32606219, CE
Kucharski, Albert, S/Sgt., 32465930, SC
Kuss, Frederick C., Pfc., 35526245, CE
Kutasiewicz, Stanley P., Pvt, 36295211, CE

- L -

La Balbo, Charles A., Pvt., 32539483, SC
La Neve, Gilbert, Pfc., 12183179, SC
La Polla, Louis R., T/3, 31104464, SC
Lacy, John N., Pvt., 39195545, CE
Laine, Elmer J., Pvt., 39321233, CE
Laliberte, Wilfred A., Pvt., 31190987, AC

Lam, Millard H., Pvt., 33538732, CE
Lambert, Hugh C., Pfc., 34623502, CE
Landry, Wilbert, Pvt., 38483000, CE
Lang, Albert E., Pfc, 11130750, AC
Langham, George H., 1 Lt., 0-789183, AC
Langnas, Robert, Pfc., 13153644, AC
Langone, John F., Pfc., 32539513, SC
Lanham, Leroy G., Pvt., 35750375, AC
Lanier, Henry O., Cpl., 18127231, AC
Lanier, Raymond K., Pvt., 39906559, CE
Lanza, Louis A., Pfc., 32773758, AC
Larimore, William L., Pfc., 35499108, AC
Larner, Arthur L., Sgt, 19083465, AC
Larsen, John W., 1/Sgt, 39388030, SC
Larson, Herman F., Cpl., 36222634, AC
Lazar, Morton N., 2.Lt., 0-1003781, AC
Leach, Fred H., 2 Lt., 0-1105602, CE
Leary, Alvin H., Pfc., 39829930, MC
Lee, William F., Pvt, 34385501, SC
Lee, Willie, T/4, 39036545, CE
Leech, Elmer L., Pvt., 35528296, CE
Lehnert, Peter E. Jr., Pvt., 35057187,
Lelonek, Stanley M., M/Sgt, 32738559, CE
Lemmon, Dudley, Pfc., 38203840, AC
Lerand, Clyde R., Cpl., 36282081, AC
Lerner, Semour, T/4, 32539520, SC
Lescault, Dominique D., S/Sgt., 31201537, CE
Levin, Benjamin, Pfc., 33477155, CE
Lewandowski, Edward M., Pvt., 36743239, CE
Lewis, L.J., T/5, 34505441, CE
Liles, Claude F., T/5, 37496154, CE
Lill, Edward G., Pfc., 12168236, AC
Lindberg, Arthur E., Pfc., 32863877, AC
Little, Benjamin A. Jr., T/4, 34612470, CE
Littman, Arthur, Pfc., 32710557, AC
Lo Balbo, Charles A., Pvt., 32539483, SC
Lofman, Alexander, Pvt., 36558305, CE
Loft, Russell E., T/5, 32679546, CE
Logiodice, Pasqual J., Pfc., 31280731, CE
Longo, Ernest, Pvt., 31291808, CE

Loos, Everett W., Pvt., 36291484, CE
Lopez, Cecelio B., T/5, 39276509, CE
Loudermilk, Revil, Pvt., 36853754,
Lowy, Reginald J., Pvt., 16120077, AC
Luccardi, Frank I., T/5, 31129837, CE
Ludeman, Merwin E., Cpl., 37319592, AC
Lukasevicius, Lawrence, Cpl., 31074463, AC
Lunday, Billy L., Cpl., 38338559, CE
Lundy, Donald E, Pfc., 33434556, AC
Lurie, Leonard, Cpl., 12061376,
Lynn, Ermal R., Pfc., 35497704, AC

- M -

Mabe, Ray D., Pvt., 14191030, SC
Mabie, Guy H., Pvt., 36484007, AC
Mac Millan, Thomas E., Pvt., 17051624, AC
Mac Skimming, Robert W., Pfc., 12165518, SC
Macaluso, Sam, T/4, 36434879, MC
Magee, James H., Pfc., 34625469, CE
Maguschak, John P., Pvt., 33605986, AC
Mahon, Vincent J., Pvt., 7021236, AC
Mahoney, James T., Pfc., 36632034, CE
Mainville, Raymond J. Jr., Pfc., 31254524, AC
Malena, Joseph, Cpl., 33290189, AC
Malott, Elmer L., Pvt., 35729366, AC
Maltesi, Gaetano R., T/5, 12165507, SC
Mann, Clyde R., Pfc., 36613187, CE
Manos, John G., Pfc., 34407485, AC
Markey, Cyril H., Cpl., 33496911, CE
Marshall, Lindon R., Pfc., 33190327
Martin, Archie A., Cpl., 16142649, AC
Martin, Clifford, Cpl., 16076425, AC
Martin, Walter M., Pvt., 13034726, INF.
Martin, William T., Pvt., 32381529, AC
Martinez, Jose E., Pvt., 38349726, CE
Masias, Louis B., Pfc., 38410611, CE
Mastroianni, Carmine A., Sgt., 32624879, AC
Mattox, Ormand A., Pvt., 37478381, INF.

Mawe, Maurice J., T/3, 38005111, AC
Mayer, Jay R., Pfc., 39460938, CE
Mazanka, Walter J., T/5, 36555153, CE
Mc Cabe, Forrest E., Pfc., 36328048, AC
Mc Cammon, George, Pvt., 37577484, INF.
Mc Carley, Kenneth R., Cpl., 35647435, CE
Mc Clung, Glenn E., Pvt., 35658108, AC
Mc Combs, Bernard L., Cpl., 35622900, CE
Mc Conchie, Alden, Cpl., 36613164, CE
Mc Cormack, Harold, Sgt., 35682742, CE
Mc Daniel, Raymond C., Sgt., 6630574, INF.
Mc Daniell, Chester, T/5, 32466040, SC
Mc Donald, Harry S., Sgt., 19125965, CE
Mc Donald, John C., Cpl., 32580472
Mc Dowell, Walter L., Sgt., 20508721, INF.
Mc Faull, Christopher F., Pvt., 34234143, CE
Mc Gill, Carl C., Cpl., 33574618, CE
Mc Gill, Charles A., Sgt., 32449089, AC
Mc Gill, John G., Cpl., 34575043, INF.
Mc Grath, Cornelius J., Pvt., 33596148, INF.
Mc Holland, Silas, Pfc., 38326407, CE
Mc Irvin, Wayne D., Sgt., 39246340, INF.
Mc Kelvey, John T., 2 Lt., 0-1108847, CE
Mc Keon, William R., Pvt., 12133697, SC
Mc Kinney, Raymond L., Pvt., 38449413,
Mc Laughlin, Francis E., Sgt., 33186929, AC
Mc Mullen, Cloyd H., Pvt., 33758691, INF.
Mc Nally, Jesse J., Pvt., 37496751, CE
Mc Naughton, Robert D., Cpl., 33403285, CE
Mc Nerney, Francis J., S/Sgt, 32553052, AC
Meacham, Robert L., Pfc., 35681752, AC
Measkey, Vernon E., Cpl., 33162662, AC
Mecey, Harold L., Pfc., 39847792, AC
Mechlin, Lloyd H., Pfc., 15011986, CE
Meeks, Melvin F., Pvt., 37493888, CE
Meranda, Marvin R., T/5, 39120208, CE
Meuller, Edgar H., Sgt., 38034351, INF.
Michael, Davis F., T/4, 34611358, CE
Middaugh, Frank E., T/5, 35622888, CE
Migliore, Pacifico A., Pfc., 31280724, CE

Migliorino, Joseph O., Pvt., 12165326, SC
Miller, Eugene D., T/5, 39460971, CE
Miller, Jackson B., T/5, 34506093, CE
Mirosavich, John, Pvt., 35529236, CE
Mitchell, Charles J., Cpl., 15323962, AC
Moe, Willie, Pfc, 39324830, CE
Mokrovich, Joseph, Pvt., 35606241, INF.
Mollela, Joseph T., T/5, 32446893,
Molnar, John G., Pvt., 32540771, SC
Molock, William C., Pvt., 34765250, INF.
Montana, Michael S., Sgt., 31275310, CE
Montgomery, George L., T/5, 12172058, SC
Moon, John I., Pvt., 36721706, CE
Moore, Boyd E., Sgt., 20726373,
Moore, John C., Pvt., 11095722, CE
Morelli, Alfred F., Pvt., 33679166, AC
Morelli, Joseph P., Pfc., 31328019, CE
Moreno, Ignacio G., Pvt., 37459339, CE
Morgan, William L., Sgt., 33351190, INF.
Morrison, Guy W., Cpl., 34490720, CE
Morvay, Lawrence L., Pvt., 32539403, SC
Moyers, Douglas R., Pvt., 33648187, INF.
Mrazek, John G., Pvt., 37612381, INF.
Mullins, Elmer E., Pfc., 34730681, AC
Murnan, Albert W., Cpl., 36459499,
Musial, Benney, Sgt., 32873195,
Music, Denver, Pfc., 35648531, CE
Myercheck, Tony P., Pvt., 35306553,

- N -

Narcaroti, Fred, Pvt., 36340260, SC
Neal, James M., Pvt., 34518065, SC
Negy, Albert A., Pvt, 12182048, SC
Nelms, Benny L., Pvt., 35681933, CE
Nelson, Archie E., Pvt, 36295206, CE
Nelson, Douglas O., Pfc, 39906592, CE
Nelson, Elwyn R., Pvt, 36295208, CE
Nelson, Emil A. Jr., Pvt., 32848233, INF.
Nelson, Homer G., Pfc., 37654148,

Nelson, Louis, Sgt, 32567909, SC
Newton, Irby L., Pvt., 34666734, CE
Nichols, Harry, Cpl., 38325680, CE
Nick, Gilbert L., Pfc., 33562582, AC
Nicks, Orvil R., Pvt., 19112957, CE
Niemiec, Marion A., Pfc., 36722023, CE
Niezgoda, Leon C., Pvt., 36613147, CE
Nixson, Edmund R, Cpl., 18077872, AC
Noble, Arthur, T/5, 35682894, CE
Nobles, T.J., Pvt, 38370823, CE
Nolan, John P. Jr., Pfc., 39117730, AC
Northcutt, Bernard L., S/Sgt., 37142736, AC
Norton, Edward P., Pvt., 12025167, AC
Norwood, Clarence, Pfc., 33519289,
Nowicki, John E., Cpl., 36507801, AC
Nugent, Buford C., Sgt., 6250477, INF.
Nugent, Joseph F., Pvt., 32278198, AC
Nulton, Clifford S., Pfc., 33458874, CE

- O -

O'brien, Henry J., Pvt., 32164182, CE
O'brien, John T., Pvt., 32791072, CE
O'neill, James J. Jr., Pvt., 32912710, INF.
Oaks, Russel E., Sgt., 13145867, AC
Oates, Paul E., Pfc., 34680180, SC
Ocel, Frank J. Sr., Cpl., 33418466, CE
Ogden, Orville L., Pfc., 36613198, CE
Oliver, Raymond L., Pvt., 38370599, CE
Olsen, Andrew W., Sgt., 32486665, CE
Olson, Howard E., Cpl., 36241398, AC
Orr, Calvin L., Pvt., 38446232, CE
Ortega, Panfilo, Pvt., 38439992, INF.
Osborn, Donald I., T/5, 37397540, CE
Osborne, Jack, T/5, 35673889,
Ostman, Arnold M., Pvt., 37558370, INF.
Owen, William A., Pvt., 34035988, CE
Owens, John E., Cpl T15, 37409570, CE

-P -

Pace, Robert F. Jr., T/4, 34370694, SC
Palmer, Earnie L. Jr., Cpl., 14177927, AC
Pantellich, Ralph, Pvt., 36568063, CE
Parent, Wilfred, Sgt., 31081777, AC
Parrish, Forrest R., Pvt., 33539778, CE
Parsons, Denver, Pvt., 35647460, CE
Partin, Raymond P., T/5, 34505802, CE
Pasagoli, Louis A., Cpl., 32539622, SC
Paslowski, Andrew, Pfc., 32865067, AC
Patterson, Mc Glothan L., T/5, 38445281, CE
Patterson, Richard B., Pvt., 35599292, CE
Patton, Ellery D., Pvt., 32873907, INF.
Paul, Joseph A., T/5, 39271841, CE
Pawlik, Eugene F., Pvt., 36723968, CE
Payne, Archie E., Cpl., 37291836, AC
Peacock, John J., T/Sgt., 7002521, AC
Pechart, John E., Sgt., 33496896, CE
Peckron, Harry H., Pvt., 37412901, CE
Peiser, Harold E., Pfc., 12193090, AC
Pelkey, Edward W., Pvt., 31254529, CE
Perkins, Warren B., T/5, 39462899, CE
Perry, Arley J., Cpl., 35624848,
Peters, Odus, T/4, 34440580,
Peterson, Frank A., Pfc., 33575967, CE
Peterson, Morley D., Pfc., 39906759, CE
Phillips, Albert E., Pfc., 39397745, AC
Phillips, James E., T/5, 36633354, CE
Philpotts, James R., Pvt., 33535744, CE
Piekarz, Joseph S., Pvt., 32889077, INF.
Pirtle, Willie L., T/5, 36440832, CE
Pisinski, Joseph J., T/4, 32568119, SC
Poole, John, Pvt., 35304611, AC
Poore, Norris A., Pfc., 31268098, CE
Pope, Harlem D., Pvt., 34681707, CE
Porter, George R., Pvt., 33720281, CE
Poteet, Jesse W., Pfc., 34505421, CE
Potocnik, Joseph G., Pvt., 33418443, CE
Potryszyn, Edward, T/5, 12165521, SC
Poucher, Burton G., T/4, 12172023, SC

Prescott, William F. Jr., Sgt., 34385568, AC
Priddy, Benjamin, Maj., 0-175081, CE
Priest, William M., Pvt., 34801139, INF.
Prock, Ernest L., Pfc., 373368643, AC
Puchalski, Stanley J., Pfc., 36630861, CE
Pyeatt, Roy D., Pvt., 38344921, CA
Pyne, Thomas P., Pvt., 31137467, AC

- Q -

Quetu, Alfred L., Pvt., 39276519, CE

- R -

Ramos, Norberto R., Pvt., 38143356, CE
Ramos, Phillip R., Pvt., 32825900, AC
Rauch, Leonard S., Sgt., 32301028, AC
Ray, George W., S/Sgt., 34493503, CE
Ray, Herman B., Pfc., 34506206, CE
Rayburn, Herbert E., Pvt., 35647660, CE
Reagle, Merl H., Pvt., 32487247, CE
Reber, Edwin M., Sgt., 32236864, AC
Reeves, Arthur J., Cpl., 16075901, AC
Reid, William P., Sgt., 36584245, AC
Reifschenider, Charles, Cpl., 36319725, AC
Reines, Eli, Cpl., 11110174, AC
Reinl, John W., S/Sgt., 33226891, AC
Resler, Robert D., Cpl., 13112029, AC
Reznicek, Frank J., Pvt., 38436107, AC
Rey, Frederick C.J., T/4, 33496864, CE
Ridgeway, Harry F., Pvt., 35749252, CE
Riley, Robert E., Pvt., 11070215, AC
Rinaldi, James P., Pfc., 31328753, AC
Rindfuss, Paul S., Pvt., 32474105, AC
Rinkus, Vincent G., Pvt., 32753873, AC
Riondino, Lewis A., Sgt., 32271871, AC
Rison, Myron R., Cpl., 35620036, CE
Rittenhouse, William A., Sgt., 12133700, SC
Rives, Lynn D., Pvt., 36448001, CE
Roback, Nathan, Pfc., 32539737, SC
Roberts, Finis J., Sgt., 18166388, AC

Roberts, Harry T., 1/Sgt., 34315532, CE
Robey, Theodore W., Pvt., 33201592, AC
Robison, Eddie H., Pfc., 37409304, CE
Rodgers, John L., Pfc., 32568310, SC
Rodriguez, Manuel A., Pvt., 38217821, CE
Roethel, Karl J., S/Sgt., 32318331, CE
Rogers, Phillp A., T/5, 32606287, CE
Rojas, Rodolfo, Pfc., 38217750, CE
Roland, Alphus R., Cpl., 18182429, AC
Rose, Ezra E., Pvt., 39193926, CE
Rosen, Harry, Pvt., 32695882, CE
Rosen, Joseph, Cpl., 13151774, AC
Rosenberg, Howard H., Pvt., 32865998, SC
Ross, James F., Cpl., 33280987, AC
Rossetti, Walter, Pvt., 33599256, CE
Rossmell, Henry J., Pvt., 32465362, AC
Rousseau, Roland, E., 31111115, T/SGT
Rutherford, James E., Pfc., 39615352, CE

- S -

Saccomana, William J., T/5, 32568351, SC
Salamone, Henry P., S/Sgt., 31152534, CE
Salopek, Pete, Sgt., 35398960, AC
Salvin, Henry J., Pvt., 33465421, SC
Sanow, Harvey, S/Sgt., 32144183, AC
Satterfield, Clifford R., S/Sgt., 31122875, SC
Schlaback, Ferris D., T/5, 36542334, CE
Schmid, Earl A., Pfc., 35795357, AC
Schneider, William J., Pvt., 36558052, CE
Schnell, Charles O., T/4, 31275858, CE
Schroeder, Harold R., Sgt., 36282338, CE
Schuh, Phillip E., Sgt., 32689226, AC
Schultz, Raymond E., Pvt., 33460238, CE
Seaman, William I., Pfc., 12172037, SC
Seavy (Seavey), Myron B., 1 Lt., 0-1103402, CE
Seidel, Max H., S/Sgt., 37415141, AC
Seigel, Leon, Pvt., 32415075, AC

Semand (Somond), Edward J., 1/Sgt., 36543436, CE

Seyerle, George C., Pvt., 33672673, AC

Shambis, Deloss H., T/5, 37466892, SC

Sharp, Paul L., Pfc., 38326043, CE

Shefulski, Peter P., Pvt., 32504173, AC

Shekell, Charles H., Pfc., 38453404, CE

Shelton, Horace E., Pvt., 38305332, CE

Shepherd, Odell, Pfc., 33562553, AC

Shilkus, Fred C., Private, 36722540, SC

Shoemaker, Ruby R., Pvt., 38369097, CE

Shull, Kenneth H., 2 Lt., 0-579226, AC

Siarkowski, Ervin E., Pvt., 35542765, CE

Sienko, Fred T., T/5, 36721686, CE

Sifuentes, Ralph V., T/5, 37494203, CE

Sink, Walton, Pvt., 36613197, CE

Sirgiovanni, Dominic, Pvt., 32700538, CE

Sistern, Ralph W., Pvt., 37654441, CE

Sitter, Ralph, Pvt., 39455310, CE

Sivulich, John, Pfc., 33460186, CE

Skvasik, Andrew J., Pvt., 12165429, SC

Slager, Justin J., Pfc., 36417850, CE

Sleeper, Lawrence J., Cpl., 31132650, AC

Sloan, Theodore, T/5, 32672745, CE

Sloat, Walter D., 2 Lt., 0-509398, SC

Smelscer, Robert Pvt., 33426133

Smith, Charles H., Pvt., 38464222, CE

Smith, Earle F., Pvt., 33553426, CE

Smith, Ernest N., Pvt., 36568162, CE

Smith, Glen E., Pvt., 36728926, CE

Smith, Harry A., T/5, 37411379, CE

Smith, Harry L., Cpl., 33553319, CE

Smith, Herman E., T/5, 34704378, CE

Smith, Hughie H., Pvt., 34625682, CE

Smith, Humphrey E., Cpl., 38394214, CE

Smith, Jasper R., Pfc., 32847486, CE

Smith, Joseph C., Cpl., 14171058, AC

Smith, Loyal H., Pvt., 36263832, SC

Smith, Paul W., Pfc., 32539439, SC

Smith, Walter E., T/5, 36297690, CE

Smith, William g. jr., Pvt., 33525476, SC

Smith, Wilson Jr., S/Sgt., 12057739, CE

Smolinsky, Peter P., Pfc., 33271005, AC

Smothermon, Choron, Pvt., 38476978, AC

Sneath, John C., Cpl., 6145722, INF.

Snedeker, Vincent B., T/5, 12133649, SC

Solomon, Herman, Pvt., 32712727, CE

Somand, Edward J., 1/Sgt., 36543476, CE

Soppe, Raymond F., Pvt., 37156293, SC

Sorrells, Everett R., Pvt., 35684495, CE

Sorrels, Walter W., T/4, 36440796, CE

Sortwell, George H., Cpl., 35567877, AC

Sosnofsky, Harry, 2nd Lt., 0-873096, AACS

Soucie, Telesphore J., Pvt., 31283142, SC

Sparacio, Jack T., Pfc., 32730604, AC

Spears, Earl J., T/5, 36441270, CE

Spears, Emerson, T/4, 32367971, SC

Spielhagen, Howard C., Pvt., 17078186, SC

Spiess, Herbert, Pfc., 32396726, AC

Spivey, Robert W., Pvt., 34763613, CE

Spruck, Hans W., Pfc., 36643706, MC

Sroka, Henry S., Pvt., 36722143, CE

Stafford, Chester E., T/5, 36440795, CE

Stankovic, Nicholas M., Pfc., 33496904, CE

Starnes, Thomas F, Pvt., 34643680, CE

Stasiak, Leon.J., Pvt., 32783131, CE

Steely, James E., T/5, 36543234, CE

Stefannice, Aldo, T/5, 32367979, SC

Stein, Edmund Cpl., 32382071

Stein, Roy A., Pfc., 36568388, CE

Stelitano, Lawrence L., Pvt., 33439432, AC

Stellato, Joseph N., Pfc., 33231674, SC

Stephenson, Chester D., Pvt., 39257087, AC

Steward, Cecil A., Pvt., 34656366, AC

Stewart, Arlie A., M/Sgt., 6076972, INF.

Stewart, Franklin M., Pfc., 325401, SC

Stinson, Ned, T/5, 37397524, CE

Straub, Arthur G., Pvt., 35684593, CE

Strole, Trenton A., S/Sgt.., 33089531, INF.

Sturges, Claude J., Pfc., 19100809, AC

Sullivan, John J., Pvt., 12182386, SC
Swanger, John M., Pvt., 35624874, CE
Sward, George S., Pvt.,]37660197, CE
Swerbinsky, Frank, Pvt., 33575107, SC
Swickey, Harry, T/4, 32537571, SC
Swobodo, Joseph J., Pvt., 15353859, AC
Szkatulski, Stanley A., Pvt., 35543892, CE

- T -

Tabor, Alfred J. Sr., Pvt., 33528666, CE
Tally, Marshall B., Pvt., 37415765, CE
Tarantola, Peter, Pvt., 32710987, CE
Tasker, Wallace, Pfc., 35746181, CE
Taylor, Harry V., Pvt., 12133648, SC
Teitelbaum, Abraham, Cpl., 12160137, AC
Terflinger, Robert F., T/5, 37494521, CE
Tester, Robert D., Sgt., 36003276,
Thell, Anton F., Cpl., 17123524, AC
Thiel, Herbert E., Pvt., 36291620, CE
Thistlewood, George W., Pvt., 32368330, SC
Thomas, Budio J., Pvt., 31291837, CE
Thomas, Joseph F., Cpl., 35007989, INF.
Thompson, Luther O., 1 Lt., 0-566909, AC
Thompson, Ross E., Pvt., 38326404, CE
Thrasher, Donald W., T/5, 35540841, CE
Throne, George W., Pvt., 33499032, CE
Thweat, Thomas D., Pvt., 34122578, CE
Tidball, Cleo L., Pvt., 37413698, CE
Tilberg, John B., T/Sgt., 32579570, AC
Tischner, Samuel P., Pvt., 32895628, AC
Tisza, John A., T/5, 32368330, SC
Tobbe, George B., Pfc., 36630673, CE
Toczylowski, Chester, T/5, 37415179, CE
Torbich, William, T/5, 33418450, CE
Tramontano, Guy J., Pvt., 32734023, CE
Trant, Russell H., S/Sgt., 37235397, AC
Trevino, Lee C., Pvt., 38114816, CE
Trimnath, Carl A., Pfc., 33569415, CE
Troutman, Raymond H., Sgt., 32139065, AC

Truax, Duane E., Pvt., 37469837, CE
Tubbs, Lloyd M., Sgt., 20726610, INF.
Tucker, Ralph W., Sgt., 18219348, AC
Turner, George H., Pvt., 35643672, SC
Tyner, Thomas O. Jr., Sgt., 14158919, AC

- U -

Ulery, John M., T/5, 33414010, CE
Underdown, George T., Pvt., 32717457, CE
Unger, Ervin W., Pvt., 37408927, CE
Unger, Frank J., Cpl., 32745693, CO
Urban, Lester J., Sgt., 26291591, CE
Uvino, Louis J., Pvt., 32805376, INF.

- V -

Vadney, Edward W., Pvt., 35643672, SC
Valentini, Vincent J., Pvt., 33131757, CE
Van Pelt, Garland L., Cpl., 18192148, AC
Van Ryn, Norman E., Cpl., 33164467, AC
Vander Giessen, John C., Pfc., 36460271, AC
Varriano, John, T/4, 12183134, SC
Vaughn, Douglass, Pfc., 15068180, MC
Veasie, John E. Jr., T/4, 11013238, SC
Vecchio, Frank, Sgt., 33111456, CE
Venclik, Emil L., Pfc., 36746216, AC
Very, Hale, 1/Sgt. 31036530, CE
Vest, Drexel, Pfc., 35798183, AC
Vidit, August, Pvt., 35527083, SC
Viehmana, Harvey C., T/5, 37411276, CE
Vilardi, Frank, Pvt., 32809127, AC
Vitnic, Frank J., T/4, 33275612, SC

- W -

Waddell, Emzie E., Pvt., 37417123, CE
Wade, William, Pvt., 35656310, AC
Wald, Weldon W., S/Sgt., 38364854, CE
Waldrep, R.B., T/5, 38340163, CE
Walker, Thomas S., M/Sg, 32272201, INF

Walters, Fred C., Pvt., 12182661, SC
Walters, Grady M. Jr., S/Sgt., 14014203, AC
Wanbaugh, William L., Pfc., 13067494, SC
Wargo, Albert S., Cpl., 33292627, AC
Wasniewski, Eugene, Pfc., 32632204, AC
Waterman, Harry E., Cpl., 11106127, AC
Webb, James R., Pfc., 339460551, CE
Weber, Thomas A., 2 Lt., 0-581327, AC
Webster, Harold C., Pfc., 33529632, CE
Weegmen, Henry, Cpl., 37177365, AC
Weidenbenner, Herbert J., T/5, 6859282, CE
Weight, Kenneth D., Cpl., 39906660, CE
Weissman, Sidney, Pvt., 32539611, SC
Welgoss, Eugene, Pvt., 33463627, INF.
Weller, Otto A., Pvt., 32367135, SC
Werber, Jack L., S/Sgt., 33446676, AC
West, Elmer N., T/4, 37405852, CE
West, Tommy B., T/4, 38445298, CE
Wheaton, Jack, Pfc., 39906571, CE
White, Harold W., T/5, 37399102, CE
Whited, Everett, T/5, 35679382, CE
Whitehead, Clinton W., T/5, 34682739, CE
Whitlowe, Jay P., 1/Sgt, 34372121, CE
Wibbelsmann, Arthur H., T/5, 35713279, CE
Wiebold, Morris G., Cpl., 17123243, AC
Wiesjahn, Walter C., Pfc., 32862294, AC
Wilder, Harry, Pfc., 11062558, SC
Wilhoite, Earle G. Jr., Pfc., 33737909, AC
Williamson, George W., Pfc., 36720827, CE
Wilpan, Seymour, Pfc., 32814209, AC
Wilson, Joseph A., Sgt., 17059182, AC
Wilson, Kenneth W., T/5, 34762425, CE
Wilson, Paul B., Cpl., 18197971, AC
Wilson, Walter O., T/4, 37494435, CE
Winingham, Earnest O., Cpl., 18198524, AC
Winters, Homer M., Pfc., 33496926, CE
Wirtanen, Onni N., Pfc., 31077425, SC
Witchey, William, T/5, 33566951, CE
Wolff, Edward A., Cpl., 12182834, AC
Wolford, Claude W., Sgt., 37424859, INF.

Wood, Miner K., 2 Lt., 0-1108428, CE
Woodruff, Walter W. Jr., Pfc., 34781871, AC
Woodstock, Francis V., Sgt., 12181341
Woody, Golden H., Pfc., 37496956, CE
Wooley, Emmitt E., Sgt., 38446280, CE
Wortman, Chester F., Pfc., 32568014, SC
Wortman, William H., Pfc., 12165536, SC

- X -

No names beginning with the letter "X"

- Y -

Yachus, Michael, Pvt., 32367984, SC
Yeager, Donald D., Cpl., 35666585, AC
Yoder, Dale R., Cpl., 33309409, AC
Young, Cecil, Pvt., 36567556,CE
Young, Clyde D., Cpl., 36568075, AC

- Z -

Zachary, Lonzo D., Pvt., 19177372, AC
Zagar, John A., T/5, 36419196, CE
Zamanigian, Martin, Pvt., 19138744, AC
Zborowski, Frank, Pvt., 36173341, CE
Zeh, Marion V., T/Sgt, 36436479, CE
Ziegenbusch, Herman H., M/Sgt., INF.
Zimmerman, Harry H., Pvt., 36440689, CE
Zura, Andrew, Pfc., 13109842, CE

List of Survivors

Branson, William R.–322nd Fighter Control
Sqdn.
Brayer, Morton F.
Breedlove, Eugene C.–AI-826-A
Breedlove, Raymond
Brewer, Robert M.–AACS
Brown, Irvin Floyd–853rd
Brown, Samuel
Bruce, Joseph L.–AACS
Bryant, Elward L.–AI-826-A
Buchanan, Edward J.–322nd Fighter Control
Sqdn.
Buchko, Andy–AI-826-A
Buck, Noah D.–CE
Buckler, J.M.
Budden, Douglass
Burlingame, Schuyler W.–853rd Eng Bn.
Burris, Charlie C.–CE
Burton, Lt. Charles E.*–322nd Fighter
Control Sq.

- C -

Caffrey, Lt. Edward F.–AACS
Cain, Plemon C.–CE
Callery, John R.–AC
Calvert, Calvin E.–322nd Fighter Control
Sqdn.
Calvin, John J.–AC
Campbell, Walter C.–322nd Fighter Control
Sqdn.
Canney, John–AI-826-A
Cantner, Paul I.–CE
Carrano, Ralph L.–31st Signal Corps
Carter, Lloyd
Carty, Fordyce–853rd Engineer Aviation Bn.
Casas, Jose V.–CE
Caskey, William R.–AI-826-A
Castaneda, Henry L.–Med. Corps
Castro, Pascual–AI-826-A

Cherry, Russell D.–AC
Childress, Wilson P.–AI-826-A
Chism, Sgt. Charles Franklin*–44th Portable
Surgical Hospital
Christensen, Harold J.–322nd Fighter
Control Sqdn.
Christiansen, William K.–AACS
Clancy, Charles R.–AC
Clonts, James–AI-826-A
Coakley, Lt. Louis G.–853rd Engineer
Aviation Bn.
Cochran, Joseph J.–CE
Coen, Earl G.–AI-826-A
Cohen, Stanley–322nd Fighter Control Sqdn.
Coleman, Phil
Confer, Joseph R.–AACS
Constantino, Anthony–CE
Coon, Harold*
Corbin, Alfred V. Jr.–AI-826-A
Costello, Raymond–31st Signal
Costello, Steve–322nd Fighter Control Sqdn.
Covey, Robert L.–AI-826-A
Coy, Wayne L.–AI-826-A
Crenshaw, Charles B.–AACS
Crivaro, Eugene
Crump, Rodney B., Jr–AI-826-A
Cudak, Anthony
Cullings, Harry M.–AI-826-A
Cummings, Charles–AC
Curles, Joel W.*–AI-826-A
Cuyler, Benjamin

- D -

Daleski, Daniel D.–AI-826-A
Dankert, Robert
Davenport, George A.–AI-826-A
Davis, Alva–853RD Eng. Bn.
Davis, Donald J–CE
Deese, J.C.–CE

Del Mastro, Philip–31st Sig. Corps
Della-Calce, Louis D.–AACS
De Rose, William
De Rouen, Elwood J–31st Sig. Corps
Deyarmon, Elwood W.–853rd Eng. Bn.
Destefano, Bernard E.–AACS
Diana, Manuel*–31st Sig. Corps
DiBenedetto, Alfred J.–853rd Eng. Bn
Dickerson, Joseph*–31st Sig. Corps
Diehl, Forrest
Difalco, Joseph–31st Sig. Bn.
Di Lorenzo, Joseph V.–AC
DiMarcello, Uresto J.–322nd Fighter Control
   Sqdn.
Doberstein, Walter R.–AI-826-A
Doherty, Louis E.–AACS
Dombroski, Anthony–CE
Donnelly, Gerald–AACS
Donovan, Kenneth P.–AACS
Doyle, Thomas A.–AC
Drajewicz, Stanislaw*–322nd Fighter Control
   Sqdn.
Drust, John B.–853rd Eng. Bn.
Dunbar, Robert H.–31st Sig. Bn
Dunmore, Frederick W.–CE
Durham, William H.*–853rd Eng. Bn.

- E -

Earhart, Richard E.–AI-826-A
Eckler, Henry C.–AI-826-A
Edwards, Charles S.–CE
Edwards, Greg
Ellis, Thomas L.–AC
Ellison, Charles W.–AI-826-A
Emson, Bob
Engelbert, Robert P.*–CE
Epifano, Ray–31st Sig. Corps
Epstein, Samuel P.–853rd Eng. Bn
Ertl, Anthony G.–CE

Evans, Gay
Evans, Calvin, Sr.

- F -

Farrell, Robert E.–Med. Corps
Fell, Ralph A.–322nd Fighter Control Sqdn.
Fehler, Lloyd C.–AI-826-A
Ferguson, Leonard
Ferguson, Richard–AACS
Fern, Roy H.–322nd Fighter Control Sqdn.
Fetsko, Andy–31st Sig. Corps
Fetterman, Russell E.–AI-826-A
Fievet, John–AI-826-A
Filbrun, Robert G.–Med. Corps
Filipchick, Joseph–AACS
Finch, Charles F.–AACS
Fiorentino, Joseph A.–AACS
Firstman, Robert
Firstman, Rubin–AACS
Fish, William (Ham)*–31st Sig. Corps
Fitzgerald, Kenney
Fitzgerald, Thomas W.–AI-826-A
Flamand, Leo J.–CE
Flath, Chester A.*–AI-826-A
Flick, Paul–31st Sig. Corps
Floyd, Mayford–CE
Flowers, Benjamin L.*–AI-826-A
Fodor, James E.–322nd Fighter Control Sqdn.
Fonte, Vincent J.–AI-826-A
Forcier, Hollis E.–322nd Fighter Control
   Sqdn.
Fortinberry, Henry A.–AI-826-A
Forwood, William M. Jr.–CE
Fouhy, Charles E Jr.*–AI-826-A
Fowler, Bill
Frank, Allan J*–Co. B 853rd
Frazier, John C.–AI-826-A
Freeman, Donald A.–AI-826-A

Freeman, Gharon O.–853rd Engineer
Aviation Bn.
Fremuth, Edward–CE
Freidman, Sol (also Friedman)–AACS
Fridley, Ira V.–853rd Eng. Bn.
Friend, Gilbert–AI-826-A
Frinsko, Frank Jr.–322nd Fighter Control
Sqdn.
Frolich, Col. A.J.–CE
Funicello, Joseph D.–853rd Eng. Bn.
Furler, Walter H.–AACS

- G -

Gaal, Julius M.–322nd Fighter Control Sqdn.
Gahwiler, Albert
Gaines, Irwin R.–AACS
Gallegos, Benito J.–CE
Galvin, John J.–AI-826-A
Gartska, Edward–853rd Engineer Aviation
Bn.
Gault, Albert W.–AI-826-A
Gautreaux, Joseph H.–CE
Geffort, Leslie*
Gentlecore, Daniel–322nd Fighter Control
Sqdn.
Geraci, Nicholas–AI-826-A
Gerrard, Kenneth
Gerstenmaier, Charles I.–AI-826-A
Giambalvo, Oasquale–CE
Gianacopoulos, John–AACS
Gibson, J.B.–AD664 A
Gikas, Gus–AACS (AI-826-A)
Gilbert, Kenneth E.–AACS
Gleason, Wesley B.–CE
Goen, Ernest G.–CE
Goettel, Donald–31st was he on Rajula
Goldberg, Robert–AACS
Goodall, Albert B. 2nd Lt.–AACS
Goodwin, Clarence H.–CE

Gordon, Earl A.–322nd Fighter Control
Sqdn.
Gough, Harold–31st Sig. Corps
Goulette, Joseph P.R.–AACS
Gouse, John B.–AC
Graham, William A.–CE
Grapentine, Charles R.–CE
Graveline, Woodrow J.–322nd Fighter
Control Sqdn.
Gray, William R.–322nd Fighter Control
Sqdn.
Grayko, John
Greeley, Donald P.–AACS
Green, David L.–AC
Green, Wiley M.–CE
Greenberg. Robert I.–AACS
Greene, Daniel–31st Sig. Bn.
Gregory, William L.–CE
Grifa, Anthony J.–322nd Fighter Control
Sqdn.
Grimes, William A.–AC
Grimm, William A.–AACS
Grimstad, Goron A.–Med. Corps
Groopman, John–AC
Gross, Sidney E.–AC
Grossnickle, Robert E.–CE
Gryn, John Jr.–CE
Guilbault, Kenneth–AACS
Gurman, Saul–AI-826-A
Gustke, Carl–AI-826-A
Guthans, Anthony H–853rd

- H -

Halasz, Gabriel–31st Sig. Corps
Hall, Donald R.–AC
Hall, Earl W.–CE
Hall, Jewel C.–CE
Haller, Jack R.–853rd Eng. Bn. (AC)
Ham, Roland Jr.–853rd Eng. Bn.

Hanna, Herbert E.*–853rd Eng. Bn
Harris, Bennett L.–AACS
Hare, Thomas L.–AI-826-A
Harrington, Harold T.–CE
Harris, Arthur W.–AI-826-A
Hart, John F.–CE
Hartzell, Richard F. Jr.–AI-826-A
Haskins, John W.–322nd Fighter Control
  Sqdn.
Hauck, Leroy1–AACS
Havern, Michael P.–322nd Fighter Control
  Sqdn.
Hayes, Robert O.–322nd Fighter Control
  Sqdn.
Hayward, Morris G.–AI-826-A
Heberle, Henry M.*–CE
Heller, Ralph E.–322nd Fighter Control Sqdn.
Henderson, William H.–CE
Herrington, Harry T.–CE
Hewitt, Clifford A.–CE
Hill, Stanley J.–322nd Fighter Control Sqdn.
Himden, Hamden F.–CE
Hinderer, Larry
Hinds, Frank S.–AI-826-A
Hinton, Hugh M.–CE
Hitchcock, Lt. William P.–AACS
Hodges, Lawrence–CE
Hoffman, William (Bill)–AI-826-A
Hoke, Isadore F.–CE
Holland, Charles A.–Med. Corps
Holliman, Thomas
Hoormann, Joe W.–CE
Hopkins, George R.–AI-826-A
Horner, Richard S.–CE
Horton, Ernest–322nd Fighter Control Sqdn.
Hostvedt, John R.–AACS
Hubing, Norbert H.–853rd Eng. Bn.
Hunt, Edwin–853rd
Hunter, Dana–AACS
Hyatt, Guy H.–CE

Hyman, Arthur

- I -

Inks, Camden W. Jr.–AI-826-A

- J -

Jachim, Stanley W. (J.)–CE
Jack, Chester A.–CE
Jackman, John E.–322nd Fighter Control
  Sqdn.
Jackson, Ulys, Capt.–853rd Aviation
  Engineering Btn.
Jacobson, Roy–31st Sig. Corps
Jaffe, Abraham–31st Sig. Corps
Jamieson, John–322nd Fighter Control Sqdn.
Jesmer, Francis P.–CE
Johnson, Charles M–CE
Johnson, Roy O.–CE
Jones, Robert F.–CE
Julius, Ralph
Junno, Paavo–AI-826-A

- K -

Kadis, Abe
Kairitis, George C.–AI-826-A
Kalyan, Andrew–322nd Fighter Control
  Sqdn.
Kantner, Paul–853rd Eng. Bn.
Kaplan, Abraham I.–Med. Corps
Kautz, Emery–322nd Fighter Control Sqdn.
Keefe, D.J.
Keesee, Andrew E.–CE
Kempner, Frank–322nd Fighter Control
  Sqdn.
Kepler, Owen F.–853rd Eng. Bn.
Korslund, Arnold M.–Med. Corps
Kelder, Robert B.–Infantry
Kellert, Frank W.–AACS

Kelley, Howard T.–AACS
Kelly, Jack–CE
Kennedy, Thomas J.–AI-826-A
Kepler, Owen F.–853rd Eng. Bn
Kerns, Richard P.–AI-826-A
Kerns, William J.–853rd Eng. Bn.
Kerr, Charles B.–CE
Kiernan, Bernard J.–Med. Corps
Kiley, Eugene, T–AI-826-A
Killian, Jere C.–AACS
King, Gerald S.–AI-826-A
Kintz, Charles R.–AI-826-A
Kinzer, Robert M.–CE
Kious, Estil J.–AC
Kippel, Robert H.–322nd Fighter Control Sqdn.
Kirkpatrick, Fred–322nd Fighter Control Sqdn.
Klehm, Ellsworth C.–AC
Kramer, Vernon J.–AACS
Kramraj, Edward J.–Infantry
Krass, Joseph D.–CE
Kris, Robert J.–853rd Eng. Bn.
Kroog, Theodore–31st Sig. Corps
Krumholtz, Ambrose W.–853rd Eng. Bn.
Kuberski, Henry J.–853rd Eng. Bn.
Kubik, John T.–AACS
Kuenick, Walter E.–AI-826-A
Kuper, Charles F.–CE
Kuperstein, Julius–31st Sig. Corps
Kuchta, Fred P.–322nd Fighter Control Sqdn.
Kutchick, Joseph Jr.–853rd Eng. Av. Bn
Kuyath, David–CE

- L -

Lacy, James K.–Infantry
La Fontaine, Charles–31st Sig. Corps
Lamson, Reginald–31st Sig. Corps
Landry, Vincent J.–AI-826-A

Larned, David J.–AI-826-A
Laws, Crawford
Leary, Alvin R.–Med. Corps
Ledwith, James J.–AI-826-A
Lee, Carleton H.–CE
Lee, Milton J.–AC
Leona, Matteo H. Jr.–CE
Leonardo, Peter–31st Sig. Corps.
Levine, Harold
Levine, Saul–31st Sig. Corps.
Levenson, Albert–AI-826-A
Levy, S/Sgt Kenneth A.–CACW
Lewis, Earl*–853rd H&S Co.
Livingston, Bennett C.–CE
Lofrese, Anthony N.*–CE
Long, Cleo R.–CE
Long, John C.–322nd Fighter Control Sqdn.
Loper, James S.–CE
Lopez, Jesse H.–853rd Eng. Bn.
Lotz, Harold S.–322nd Fighter Control Sqdn.
Lundborn, Raymond A.–AI-826-A
Lunsmann, Elmer G.–Med. Corps
Luna, Alfredo–CE
Lutgring, Edwin B.–AACS
Lynch, Joseph T–AACS

- M -

Macias, Jesus M.–CE
Mahoney, Freeman D.–AACS
Majkszak, Arthur J.–AACS
Macaluso, Sam–Med. Corps
Markiewitz, Louis–853rd Av.Bn.
Marks, Abraham M.–AACS
Martin, George A.–CE
Martin, George Ray
Martin, Raymond M.–AI-826-A
Martin, Martin R.–AC
Martinex, Fred–CE

Martino, Nicholas–31st Signal Heavy
   Construction Bn.
Martocke, George M.–AI-826-A
Marx, Marvin*
Mason, Wallace–33rd Infantry Replacement
   Bn.
Mayhew, Clarence F. Jr.–CE
Mayville, Kenneth L.–AACS
McCarter, Roy Clell*–853rd
McCarthey, Vincent J.–322nd Fighter Control
   Sqdn.
McCoy, John D.–AACS
McCune, John O. Jr.–AACS
McDermott, William S.–AACS
McFall, Max Phillip–A1826-A
McGrane, Paul J.–Infantry
McGuire, Mannie L.–AC
McKee, William
McKee, James
McKinney, Ebert (Elbert H.)–322nd Fighter
   Control Sqdn.
McKinnon, Arlin D.–AACS
McDermott, William S.–AACS
McLennan, John J.–AACS
McQuatters, Joseph A.–RH705AAA
Merker, Tom
Messina, John
Meyer, Arthur W.–AI-826-A
Meyers, James C.–322nd Fighter Control
   Sqdn.,
Michaels, Walter (Also reported as killed)–
   AI-826-A
Michnofsky, Thomas–AC
Middleton, Daniel B.–AACS
Mikels, Billie–AACS
Mikolajczak, Walter J.–AC
Miles, Herald E.–AI-826-A
Millar, Nelson M.–CE
Miller, Mervin L.–853rd Engineer Aviation
   Bn.

Miller, Irvin J.–AACS
Miller, Jesse L.–322nd Fighter Control Sqdn.
Milner, William
Mikels, Billie–AACS
Minner, Paul H.–AACS
Mitchell, George R.–AACS
Molek, Leon C.–CE
Monger, James R.–AACS
Montgomery, Hulon H.–CE
Moore, Howard–322nd Fighter Control
   Sqdn.
Morelli, Victor E.–31st Sig. Corps
Morgan, Philip–Med. Corps
Morocco, Joseph*–31st Sig. Corps
Morosoff, William–AACS
Morrison, Raymond J. Jr.
Mortenson, Glen
Moskowitz, David P.–AACS
Mosteller, Frederick–31st Sig. Corps
Mouse, Harmon K.–322nd Fighter Control
   Sqdn.
Muchnick, Simon
Mulvaney, Robert J. P.–Med. Corps
Mountain, Gilbert N. Jr.–Med. Corps
Myers, Jim–322nd Fighter Control Sqdn.

- N -

Nadel, Morris
Namerow, Nathan–31st Sig. Corps
Natoli, Joseph–Infantry
Neal, Clarkey L.–853rd Eng. Bn.
Neff, Robert H.–322nd Fighter Control Sqdn.
Neilson, Donald H.–AACS
Neveu, Robert P.–AI-826-A
Newman, Ivan R–853rd Eng. Bn.
Ney, Walter–AI-826-A
Nichols, Raymond D.–CE
Noh, Robert P.–322nd Fighter Control Sqdn.
Norrod, William A.–AACS

- O -

Obra, Richard–853rd Eng. Bn.
Ohly, William–CE
O'Brien, Carl J.–AI-826-A
O'Brien, Bill–CE
O'Conner, Donald T.–AACS
O'Neal, C.L. "Bus"–853rd Eng. Bn.
Orsa, John Sr.–Infantry
Orsegno, Pasquale W.–Infantry
Osowski, Leonard–AC
Overstreet George D.–322nd Fighter Control Sqdn.
Overton, Henry W.–322nd Fighter Control Sqdn.

- P -

Paciello, Samuel D.–AACS
Pacheco, Macario A.–31st Sig. Corps
Palluth, Ervin W.–AI-826-A
Palmer, Warren G.–Infantry
Panion, Frederick*–AI-826-A
Parelli, Alphonse W.
Parker, Daniel H.–AACS
Parmentier, A.J.
Partelow, William K.–AI-826-D
Paskowski, John–31st Sig. Corps
Pawlowski, Edward J.–322nd Fighter Control Sqdn.
Payne, Arnold E.–322nd Fighter Control Sqdn.
Pelcher, Frank F.–CE
Paulseen, Kenneth S.–AC
Peach, Richard H.*–31st Sig. Corps
Peck, Maynard
Percle, Corbett J.–AI-826-A
Peterson, Sharon
Pezoldt, David J.–AI-826-A
Pezoldt, Joseph D.–AI-826-A
Phelps, Louis R.–CACW

Philion, Albert C.–322nd Fighter Control Sqdn.
Phillips, Joe R.–AC
Piquard, Eugene H.–31st Sig. Corps
Pitman, Herbert H.–AACS
Ploegert, Robert J.——CE
Price, Edwin A.–Infantry
Pythian, Richard J.–AI-826-A
Pope, James–31st Sig. Bn.
Popkins, Robert
Portelow, William K.–AACS
Porter, Robert J.–AACS
Porter, Kenneth R.–AACS
Porter, Virgil C.–CE
Portnoy, Abe–322nd Fighter Control Sqdn.
Powell, Harvey Housley
Procton, Albert–AACS
Prosky, Abraham (aka Procton)–AACS
Proto, Charles–AI-826-A
Pumelia, Anthony J.

- Q -

Querido, Sidney–322nd Fighter Control Sqdn.
Quick, William C.*–AI-826-A

- R -

Ragona, Peter J.–322nd Fighter Control Sqdn.
Raibley, Edgar C.–AC
Rains, Roy A. (Ray)–CE
Ramirez, Ysidoro R.–322nd Fighter Control Sqdn.
Ramsey, Buster B.–322nd Fighter Control Sqdn.
Randis, Walter A.–CE
Rawson, Roy Tyler, Jr.–31st Sig. Corps
Rees, Lewis–322nd Fighter Control Sqdn.
Reidy, James D.–AACS Air Corps
Reiman, Burton–AACS

Renzo, Anthony J.–322nd Fighter Control
    Sqdn.
Rewkowski, Leo *–AACS
Rhines, Milford–322nd Fighter Control
    Sqdn.
Rice, Herman E,–CE
Risley, Edward S,–AACS
Rives, Glen L–CE
Riwkes, Siegfried W.–322nd Fighter Control
    Sqdn.
Rockwell, William–CE
Rodrigues, Frank–322nd Fighter Control Sqdn.
Roger, Laurent J.–AI-826-A
Rodgers, John L.–AC
Rogers, John L.–AACS
Ross, Robert W.–322nd Fighter Control
    Sqdn.
Rosinski, Eugene J.–31st Sig. Corps
Rosseau, John W.–AACS
Rossetti, Paul
Rowe, James*–31st Sig. Corps
Rudnitsky, Abraham–AC
Rund, Clifford A.–AACS
Russell, William H.–322nd Fighter Control
    Sqdn.

- S -

Sacco, Eugene A.–AI-826-A
Salsman, Alfred J.–AI-826-A
Salvati, Thomas A.–322nd Fighter Control
    Sqdn.
Salzillo, Lt. William–853rd
Sammons, Floyd R.–853rd Eng. Bn.
Sanner, Albert E.–AACS
Santti, Sulo E.–CE
Sarnotsky, Seymour*–AI-826-A
Sauls, Oretus E. Jr.–322nd Fighter Control
    Sqdn.
Sawicki, Edward J.–AC

Saxon, Weldon F.–AI-826-A
Scheideler, David C.–853rd Eng. Bn.
Schoenacker, Carl E.–322nd Fighter Control
    Sqdn.
Schroeder, John F.–322nd Fighter Control
    Sqdn.
Schultz, Frank–322nd Fighter Control Sqdn.
Sears, Fred
Seidel, Jerome M.–AACS
Senne, August L.–AI-826-A
Shatto, Miles T.–322nd Fighter Control Sqdn.
Shaw, Lt. Robert B.*-853 Engr Bn
Shelton, Charles
*Sher, Pvt. Sidney
Sherman, Hyman–AACS
Sherrill, Robert L.–AI-826-A
Sherwood, William L.–322nd Fighter Control
    Sqdn.
Shimon, John–322nd Fighter Control Sqdn.
Shimp, Jake–AI-826-A
Shufelt, Lyle C.–AI-826-A
Sidoti, Peter R. 1–AC
Silver, George M.–AACS
Simmons, Ernest J.–AI-826-A
Sinare, Anthony–AACS
Skewis, Edwin–31st Sig. Corps
Slater, Maxwell
Slujnski, John–AI-826-A
Smart, Frederick B.–322nd Fighter Control
    Sqdn.
Smith, Edward H.–CE
Smith, George W.–322nd Fighter Control
    Sqdn.
Smith, John W.–AACS
Smith, John L.–AI-826-A
Smith, Raymond A.–322nd Fighter Control
    Sqdn.
Smith, Robert E. Jr. #14,178,057–AI-826-A
Smith, Robert E. Jr. #32,431,825–AC
Smith, Lt. Winton R.–AACS

Smutney, Ludwik*
Snoddy, Sam
Snyder, Louis E.*–CE
Sotomayer, Perfecto S.–CE
Specter, Lt. Sam I.–AACS
Speicher, James O.–322nd Fighter Control
  Sqdn.
Spruck, Hans W.–Med. Corps
Spurbeck, George–853rd Aviation Eng. Btn.
Spurlock, Clifford M.–CE
St. John, Ronald P.–AACS
Stafford, Charles E.–853rd Eng. Bn.
Stankiewicz, Walter F.–853rd
Stanton, Leo F.–322nd Fighter Control Sqdn.
Stauffer, John
Steenhout, William G.–853rd Eng. Bn.
Steele, Douglas
Steele, Richard H.–AI-826-A
Stefenoni, Alfred J.–322nd Fighter Control
  Sqdn.
Steiner, Richard F–322nd Fighter Control Sqdn.
Stevens, Kenneth M.–AI-826-A
Stevens, Robert C. Jr.–AACS
Stewart, Charles V.–31st Signal Construction
  Bn.
Stewart, James P.–CE
Stone, George P., Jr.–AACS
Stout, Marshall R.–AI-826-A
Straty, George–AACS
Steenhout, Frank–853rd
Stricker, Gilbert F.–AACS
Stroud, Harold H.–853rd Eng. Bn.
Strout, Marshall–AI-826-A
Sumeral, Delton*–853rd Engineer Aviation Bn.
Sullivan. Francis J.*–31st Sig. Heavy
  Construction Bn
Sullivan, Gerald D. 1–AC
Swain, Lt. John W.–AACS
Swasey, William G.–CE

- T -

Tassone, Dominic V.–AI-826-A
Tattelman, Paul–322nd Fighter Control Sqdn.
Taylor, Paul M.–322nd Fighter Control Sqdn.
Taylor, Raymond Cecil—T/5, 853rd
Taylor, Roy–AI-826-A
Taylor, Jacob W.–853rd Eng. Bn
Teague, Thomas B.–CE
Templeton, Lt. William C. Jr.–AACS
Toellner, Walter E.–322nd Fighter Control
  Sqdn.
Thomas, James–853rd Eng. Bn.
Thomas, Vernie L.–AI-826-A
Thomas, Wilbur–AI-826-A
Thompson, Charles L.–CE
Toellner, Walter E.–322nd Fighter Control
  Sqdn.
Tomasino, Arthur A.–322nd Fighter Control
  Sqdn.
Tomaszewski, Roman M.–AI-826-A
Tominia, Carmelo
Tompkins, Charles F.–322nd Fighter Control
  Sqdn.
Torcerice, Charles (aka Tortice)
Torres, Agapito S.*–CE
Townes, Charles F.–AC
Trammel, Howard G.–CE
Trapanese, Joseph–853rd Eng. Bn.
Tresler, Floyd C.–322nd Fighter Control
  Sqdn.
Truckenbredt, Edgar W.–Infantry
Trywusch, Myron J.–322nd Fighter Control
  Sqdn.
Tsouflou, George

- U -

No names beginning with the letter "U"

- V -

Valdez, Jesus F.–853rtd Eng. Bn.
Van Brunt, Frank H.–31st Sig. Corps.
Van Sickle, Lt. Don P.–853rd
Vandentop, Albert
Vannest, Kenneth H. (R.)–AC (322nd Fighter Control Sqdn.)?
Vangeloff, August–322nd Fighter Control Sqdn.
Vangi, John*–31st Sig. Corps
Vaughn, Douglas–Med. Corps
Ventresca, Nick
Vigil, Agapito–853rd Eng. Bn.
Vinitzky, Herman–322nd Fighter Control Sqdn
Visser, Richard
Vogler, Richard C.–322nd Fighter Control Sqdn.

- W -

Wagner, Gilbert A.–CE
Waldon, Jack C.–322nd Fighter Control Sqdn.
Warneke, Erwin H.–AI-826-A
Warren, William H.–322nd Fighter Control Sqdn.
Wary, Joe–31st Sig. Corps
Weber, Aaron–322nd Fighter Control Sqdn.
Weisbord, Rubin (Weisbrod) AC
Westphal, James L.–322nd Fighter Control Sqdn.
Wheeler, Forrest W.–322nd Fighter Control Sqdn.
Wheeler, Sgt. James E.–RH705AAA
White, Louie L.–322nd Fighter Control Sqdn.
Whitesel, Richard H.–322nd Fighter Control Sqdn.
Wilde, Cap't Arnold R.–853rd Eng. Bn.
Wilde, Don R.–853rd Eng. Bn.

Wilde, Harold L.–853rd Eng. Bn
Wilhelm, Leonard M.–CE
Willeford, Edward H.–853rd
Williams, Aubrey H.–322nd Fighter Control Sqdn.
Williams, Charles J.–31st Sig. Corps
Williams, Otho B.–AI-826-A
Williams, Shelby E.–322nd Fighter Control Sqdn.
Williamson, Jesse W.–CE
Willis, Robert K.–322nd Fighter Control Sqdn.
Wilkie, Herbert M.–AACS
Wilson, Roland L.–31st Sig. Corps
Wohl, Benson–CE
Wohlt, Norbert Edward "Nubs"*–853rd Av.Eng
Wolff, Wm Fred–31st Sig. Corps.
Woody, Robert D.–853rd Eng. Bn.
Wright, Charles

- X -

Xanthus, Peter–31st Signal Heavy Construction Bn.

- Y -

Yost, Orlo E.–31st Signal
Young, Fred
Young, James P.–CE

- Z -

Zajac, Charles M.–CE
Zediker, Ralph C.–CE
Zeller, Gilbert M.–CE
Zirkle, Donald–Infantry

1 Reported as seriously injured in action. Survival status unclear.

List of Non-American Rohna Casualties

Officers and men who lost their lives at sea due to enemy action

Europeans

G.W. Burrell	Chief Officer
A.C. Cranfield	Second Officer
J.A. Welsh	Second Engineer
J. Pugh	Fourth Engineer
J. Hulme	Junior Engineer

Indian Seamen

Muklesur Rahman x Umberali	F. Serang
Abdool Mozid x Hari Bepari	First Tindal
Gonoo Meah x Abassallee	Second Tindal
Eman Allee x Rajab Allee	Donkeyman
Abdul Latif x Chand Mian	Lampman
Habib Rahman x Tozoomeah	Iceman
Fozoo Meah x Bachoo Mohd	Oilman
Noor Bux x Abdul Meah	Oilman
Mohamed Meah x Mathy Meah	Oilman
Azizor Rohoman x Jamid Allee	Oilman
Afzal x Eman Ali	Fireman
Nehazur Rahman x Merherali	Fireman
Sharazul Huq x Hasan Ali	Fireman
Altoo Meah x Amir Ali	Coal Trimmer
Muslim Meah x Islam Meah	Coal Trimmer
Muruzali x Wazidali	Coal Trimmer
Jewa Ranchord	First Tindal
Muckan Chibba	Seacunny

Doolab Seeba	Seacunny
Makan Lalla	Seacunny
Goven Vallab	Seacunny
Vallubb Rama	Lascar
Meetha Fackeer	Lascar
Fackeer Sooka	Lascar
Valub Ranchord	Lascar
Fackeer Meetha	Lascar
Manchia Dettia	Lascar
Bhana Kalidas	Lascar
Lalla Karia	Lascar
Naroon Jadhow	Lascar
Nathoo Grandha	Lascar
Daya Kallia	Lascar
Daira Deiva	Lascar
Mohamed x Dar Buksh	Lascar
Shandar Seeba	Lascar
Purbhoo Lalloo	Lascar
Karia Goven	Lascar
Mahadeo Kallia	Lascar
Bawa Veera	Lascar
Lalloo Karia	Lascar
Ranchord Daya	Half Lascar
Surta Bihar	Topass
Sangar Chowara	Topass
F. Gomes	Storekeeper
Francis Pereira	Headwaiter
Vincent Lobo A. Lobo	Second Cook
Martin Fernandes	Pantryman's Mate
Janowal Fernandes	Baker
Louis Pinto x Anton Pinto	Assistant Baker
Justiciano Coelho	Butcher

Marian P. Coorea	Butcher's Mate
Basil Rodriques	First Pantryman
Mariano Lopes	Second Pantryman
Santan Fernandes	Pantryman's Mate
C.S. Fernandes	Chief Engineer's Boy
Jerominio N. Pais	General Servant
Mathews C. Gomes	General Servant
Caetan Francis Fernandes	General Servant
Gasper Piedade Fernandes	General Servant
Francis Fernandes	General Servant
Sabastiao Piedade	General Servant
Roque B. Fernandes	General Servant
Joaquim Rozario Godinho	General Servant
Roque Pereira	General Servant
John D'Souza	General Servant
Ignacio Francis Menezies	General Servant
Thomas Fernandes	General Servant
Antonio Manoel	General Servant
J.M. Fernandes	General Servant
S.P.A. Paes	General Servant
Francis Fernandes	Scullion
Nicolan Fernandes	Scullion
Joaquim V. Alfonso	Topass
Ignacio Fernandes	Topass
Alex D'Costa	Troop Butler
R.C. Almeida	Troop Storekeeper
J.D. Cardoso	Canteen Steward
C. D'Silva	Troop Assistant
Jose Fernandes	Troop Chief Cook
Jerome Fernandes	Troop Second Cook
Laurence Fernandes	Troop Second Cook
Caetan Collaco	Troop Third Cook

Ozario Caetan Fernandes	Troop Baker
Francisco Dias	Troop Assistant Baker
Joaquim R. Godinho	Troop Baker's Mate
Bendoo Correa	Troop Butcher
Octaviano D.M. Pinto	Troop Assistant Butcher
Verodian Fernandes	Troop Butcher's Mate
Natividade Fegueredo	Troop General Servant
Jose Domingos Fernandes	Troop General Servant
Augustino Fernandes	Troop General Servant
S. Fernandes	Troop General Servant
F. Cardina	Troop General Servant
Phillip Fernandes	General Servant
Gregory Tauro	General Servant
M.F. Cabral	General Servant
Manuel Jose Pereira	Fourth Cook
Sebastiao Fernandes	Fourth Cook
Joao Jose Timoti	Scullion
Santan Monterio	Topass
D. Baretto	Half General Servant
Anthon Baretto	Troop Third Cook
Jose Minguel Furtado	Troop Baker's Mate
Alexander Leitao	Troop Scullion
M. Antao	General Servant
R. Sequeira	Topass
A. D'Costa	General Servant
C.P. Vaz	General Servant

Ranks aboard ship

	British	Lascars
a) **Deck**	Bosun	Serang
	Bosun's Mate	Tindal
	Quartermaster	Seacunny
	Carpenter	Mistree
	Lamptrimmer	Kussab
	Able Seaman	First Class Lascar
	Ordinary Seaman	Second Class Lascar
b) **Engine Room**	Donkeyman	Serang *Note 1
	-	Tindal * Note 2
	Apprentice	Topas
c) **Saloon**	Second Steward	Butler * Note 3
d) **Catering**	Cook	Bhandary

Notes

* 1. In larger vessels, such as those of P & O, there was a European Donkeyman and the Serang was separate, but equal, petty officer.

* 2. No equivalent. The Storekeeper, who would normally be next in line to the Donkeyman, was invariably a European. The Tindal usually stood his watch with the Chief Engineer from 0800 to noon and 2000 to midnight.

* 3. In smaller vessels, such as those of the Strick Line, the Butler was also Chief Steward. He had the same rights of engagement and control over the Stewards as the Serangs had in their departments.

The list came from "Valiant Voyaging", by Hilary St. George Saunders. This book is a short history of the British India Steam Navigation in

WWII. It was first printed in London by Faber and Faber LTD in 1948 and makes for very interesting reading if you can find a copy.

Tennessee Representative Steve McManus

One evening at the May, 2007 reunion in Nashville, Tennessee, Don Dupre (USS Pioneer, AM105) struck up a conversation with a man on the elevator. It turned out that he was interested in history; in particular WWII. His name was Steve McManus and he was a Tennessee State Representative. Mr. McManus asked if he could visit the Rohna hospitality suite and talk to survivors. After spending quite a while in the suite he offered to invite a group to sit in the gallery of the state capitol building the next morning. After the Rohna group was seated, Mr. McManus asked to make an announcement to the floor of the House of Representatives. In his speech he gave the history of the Rohna and then asked the survivors to rise. The group received a very loud and sustained applause.

You can see streaming video by going to:
www.legislature.state.tn.us
This takes you to the "Welcome" page.
On the left side of the screen, click on "House".
In the drop-down menu, click on "Video Streaming".
Under "105th Broadcasts, House Sessions (1st regular session)", select the date: May 24, 2007.
It will take a minute or two for the video to start. Once it does, you can drag the "slider" (the green bar below the video) to the right. Now you can "fast-forward" to 1 hour and 34 minutes. That is the section regarding the Rohna presentation.

In June, 2007 the Rohna Organization was sent the following resolution that had been championed by Representative McManus:

State of Tennessee
House of Representatives
House Joint Resolution No. 676

A RESOLUTION to recognize and honor the survivors of the HMT Rohna for valorous service during World War II and for their commitment to honor the memory of their fallen comrades.

WHEREAS, our nation was conceived by individuals who were willing to sacrifice their personal safety and concerns to insure our individual and collective freedom; the American troops aboard the HMT Rohna, having performed above and beyond the call of duty, should be specially honored by this legislative body; and

WHEREAS, on November 26, 1943, during World War II, the British troopship, the HMT Rohna, was attacked from the air and destroyed in the Mediterranean Sea off the coast of Algeria; and

WHEREAS, the ship was part of a convoy traveling east from Oran to the Far East via the Suez Canal: the sinking of the HMT Rohna marked the first successful "hit" of a merchant vessel at sea carrying U.S. troops by a German remote-controlled, rocket-boosted bomb, thus giving birth to the "Missile Age"; and

WHEREAS, the attack resulted in the greatest loss of troops, 1,015, at sea in American history; combined with loss of the ship's crew, officers, and Red Cross workers, more lives were lost than on the USS Arizona at Pearl Harbor; and

WHEREAS, the hit was so devastating that the federal government placed a veil of secrecy upon the events of that day, and that secrecy continued for decades. Only recently were documents released under the Freedom of Information Act; thus, most families of the casualties still do not know the fate of their loved ones; and

WHEREAS, in 1995, over fifty years later, a group of survivors, next-of-kin, and rescuers, informally came together for the sole purpose of enabling the creation and dedication of a Rohna Memorial; and

WHEREAS, on Memorial Day in 1996, a monument was dedicated at Fort Mitchell National Cemetery in Seale, Alabama, to honor the memory of the 1,015 men who lost their lives in the sinking of the HMT Rohna; and

WHEREAS, four years later, the Rohna Memorial Survivors Memorial Association became more formally organized, and many of those involved with the earlier Memorial Dedication project worked diligently toward the formation of this new organization; and

WHEREAS, articles and by-laws were drawn up and the association defined its goals, which are: to continue in the search for survivors as-yet-undiscovered and the families of those who perished, so as to provide them with information they never had about the fate of their loved ones; to bring the Rohna story before the public, to honor the men who lost their lives in this incident and those on the rescue vessels who acted selflessly in their rescue efforts; and to further, by reunions and other communications, the closeness among the membership; and

WHEREAS, it is most appropriate that this General Assembly, should honor the memory and the lives of the U.S. troops who were aboard the HMT Rohna that fateful day in 1943; now, therefore,

BE IT RESOLVED BY THE HOUSE OF REPRESENTATIVES OF THE ONE HUNDRED FIFTH GENERAL ASSEMBLY OF THE STATE OF TENNESSEE, THE SENATE CONCURRING, that we honor and commend the gallant American troops who were aboard the HMT Rohna that tragic day in November of 1943; we recognize their valorous service to a grateful nation, salute their conspicuous gallantry and intrepidity during World War II, and laud the ship's heroic survivors for their stalwart commitment to honor the memory of their fallen comrades.

ADOPTED: June 11, 2007

Signed by: James O. Naifeh, Speaker of the House of Representatives
Ron Ramsey, Speaker of the Senate
Phil Bredesen, Governor
Steve McManus, Representative

978-0-595-49679-2
0-595-49679-2

Printed in the United States
150329LV00001B/113/P

9 780595 496792